TEXT BY ANNE BUTLER

PHOTOGRAPHY BY HENRY CANCIENNE

UNIVERSITY OF LOUISIANA AT LAFAYETTE PRESS
2010

University of Louisiana at Lafayette Press
P.O. Box 40831
Lafayette, LA 70504-0831
http://ulpress.org

© 2010 by University of Louisiana at Lafayette Press

Printed on acid-free paper in China by Everbest Printing Co. through Four Colour Imports, Ltd., Louisville, Kentucky.

ISBN 13 (hardcover): 978-1-887366-99-1
ISBN 10 (hardcover): 1-887366-99-7

Library of Congress Cataloging-in-Publication Data

Butler, Anne, 1944-
 Louisiana Hwy. 1 / text by Anne Butler ; photography by Henry Cancienne.
   p. cm.
 ISBN-13: 978-1-887366-99-1 (hardcover : alk. paper)
 ISBN-10: 1-887366-99-7 (hardcover : alk. paper)
1. Louisiana--Description and travel. 2. Louisiana--Pictorial works. 3.
Louisiana Highway 1 (La.) 4. Louisiana Highway 1 (La.)--Pictorial works. I.
Cancienne, Henry, 1946- II. Title. III. Title: Louisiana Highway 1. IV. Title:
Louisiana Highway One.
 F369.B97 2010
 917.6304'64--dc22
                                2010020936

Introduction

Oil platforms off the coast of Port Fourchon

Louisiana Hwy. 1, Louisiana's first complete state-wide road, sweeps up out of the Gulf like the swashbuckling pirates of old, and ends 436 miles northwest, where equally daring wildcatters tapped black gold with the first oil well over water. Along the way, it crosses through communities representing just about every culture that historically has spiced up Louisiana's gumbo heritage and history.

Now a swift superhighway traverses much the same route, but speed can never supplant the style and substance of the days when travel involved not merely a destination to be reached post-haste, but a journey whose every step was to be savored, with time to smell the irises and the roses, to sample the seafood and the meat pies, to dance to the accordions and the country fiddles, to feast the eyes on vast fields of cotton or sugarcane. From the dark,

rich, cypress-shaded bayouside battures to the red dirt hills and piney woods along the way, the route embraces architecture uniquely suited to each setting, from cozy Acadian cabins to the magnificent plantation mansions and a lifestyle to match, from the "fragrantly French" *joie de vivre* of the bayous to the austere Bible belt.

No other roadway provides such a cross-section of Louisiana life and history. LA 1 crisscrosses the state through twelve parishes—Jefferson, Lafourche, Assumption, Ascension, Iberville, West Baton Rouge, Pointe Coupée, Avoyelles, Rapides, Natchitoches, Red River and Caddo—from Grand Isle and the Port Fourchon center of deepwater oil and gas activity on the Gulf of Mexico to the Ark-La-Tex border northwest of big, bustling, industrialized Shreveport. It is the longest numbered highway in Louisiana. This connection between north and south was of such enormous importance that in its 1981 inaugural issue's feature article the state's premier magazine, full-color *Louisiana Life*, called LA 1 the ribbon that ties Louisiana together, a ceremonial sash proudly worn by the state from its right shoulder to its left hip.

While Louisiana's incredibly diverse subregions have always been divided and distinct due to cultural and linguistic differences, they were also separated by enormous transportation difficulties in the early days of the region's development. Waterways—nearly 5,000 miles of navigable streams and rivers, bayous, and canals—were the Bayou State's first highways. They created routes followed by the first roadways, often rude dirt thoroughfares that began as cow paths or foot trails and had to be built and maintained not only by the none-too-prosperous

holders of the early land grants, but also by the big concessions or plantations and smaller habitations stretching back from the riverbanks. Not until the colorful and controversial Kingfish, Huey P. Long, became governor in 1928, with his populist "Every Man A King" philosophy, was there an attempt to connect even the major settlements with paved roads.

Louisiana had a deplorable roadway system, thanks to its erosive soil, lack of durable local construction materials, and heavy rainfall and drainage problems. Improved transportation was one of Long's most important campaign planks and was considered by many to be the issue that elected him. In 1928, Louisiana had fewer than three hundred miles of concrete roads; some estimates, including a Highway Commission report cited by Long biographer T. Harry Williams, were much lower, a mere

thirty-one miles of concrete roads and sixty-five miles of asphalt, plus a bunch of disconnected gravel roads and only three major bridges in a state with the most waterways in the nation. But Governor Long implemented a flurry of bond-financed road and bridge building that placed Louisiana's highways and free bridges among the best in the country at that time.

Was it any wonder far-flung communities were isolated from each other? The patchwork of dirt and gravel or shell roads linking even major towns consisted of rutted tracks that turned into impassible quagmires after heavy rains; heavily loaded wagons and early car models became mired in the mud and could not continue their journeys until extricated by teams of mules or oxen. Said the inaugural program of Gov. Richard Leche, "It took a millionaire with the constitution of an ox to go from one place to another in the Louisiana of 1928, a millionaire who was something of a trail blazer and expert woodsman, to boot."

Of all of his accomplishments to help the downtrodden—the establishment of charity hospitals and state mental facilities, the free school books and expanded educational programs, the abolition of the poll tax and the imposing new capitol building at Baton Rouge that would be the scene of his 1935 assassination—Huey Long was most proud of his roads program. Despite problems with patronage and forced contributions to his "DE-duct box," not to mention the fact that much of the backbreaking road clearing was done with picks, shovels, and wheelbarrows through thick woods and swamps teeming with snakes and alligators, during Long's reign the state benefitted from thousands of miles of new concrete

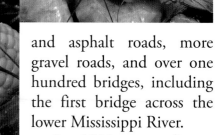

and asphalt roads, more gravel roads, and over one hundred bridges, including the first bridge across the lower Mississippi River.

In 1931, expenditures for roads and bridges totaled more than 66 percent of the state's budget, providing employment for a huge number of workers who would otherwise have had to rely on public relief during the Depression era. The roads were a godsend for planters to get their crops to markets and for the general populace trying to get anywhere at all. The trip from Shreveport to New Orleans that had required three costly nights in a hotel plus innumerable ferry tolls could now be accomplished in a single day, while the journey from Baton Rouge to New Orleans, once a day-long "nightmarish experience," took only a couple of hours.

LA 1 was called the backbone state highway, Louisiana's Main Street, along its course flirting continuously with the state's waterways—rambling along the Red River, cruising across the Cane River,

Swamp in Lower Lafourche

Crude oil wellheads, referred to as Christmas trees, dot the swampland.

arching over the Atchafalaya and meandering beside the Mississippi, with languid bayou waters lapping at its sea-level roadbed the length of Bayou Lafourche. But LA 1 actually combined several earlier piecemeal roadways. During 1915, in New Orleans, 650 interested parties met to discuss the ambitious goal of building a highway from the Gulf of Mexico to Winnipeg, Canada. Ten years later, the group celebrated, somewhat prematurely, the completion in 1924 of Louisiana's portion of what was called the Jefferson Highway; Minnesota would be the second state to complete its section of this roadway. This being Louisiana, the boastful claim of being the first state to finish its section was not entirely the gospel truth, as the road began in New Orleans and would not actually attempt to reach the gulf coast until 1931, when the highway from Golden Meadow to Grand Isle began.

In 1930, during a statewide campaign to drum up support for a gas tax to fund highway improvements, Governor Long promised concrete roads from Plaquemine to Simmesport. This swung the route of what would become LA 1 to the west bank of the Mississippi River and away from the crown jewel of Long's road-building program, the New Orleans-to-Baton Rouge Airline Highway, a long-awaited boon to automotive traffic, but a huge hazard to wildlife. Once that highway had opened to great acclaim, its shoulders were soon littered with the limp bodies of Great Horned Owls and other nocturnal creatures bewildered by bright headlights piercing the customary darkness of the depths of the swamps. As for the portion of LA 1 through Lower Lafourche, it would not be paved until 1949.

From sunrise over gulf waves to sunset on serene Caddo Lake, today LA 1 showcases Louisiana's incredible variety of terrain and cultures, from the energy and seafood industries of Cajun country, through the capital region around Baton Rouge, to the pecan orchards and piney hills of the Kisatchie National Forest area, through the unique Creole culture of Cane River/Natchitoches and Louisiana's earliest historic settlements, on up to the northwestern commercial center of Shreveport.

At present, Louisiana has more than sixty thousand miles of roads, but 25 percent of the vehicles pass along its one thousand miles of interstate highway. The occupants don't know what they're missing.

Upper LA 1 is like a roller coaster through the hills of North Louisiana.

Down the Bayou

Grand Isle

Louisiana Hwy. 1 begins just about as far south as you can go in Louisiana without being in the middle of the Gulf of Mexico. It has its inauspicious start at the east end of the tiny coastal resort of Grand Isle, Louisiana's only inhabited barrier island, seven and a half miles long and a mile across at its widest. This was the early 1800s stomping grounds of Jean Lafitte and his band of brigands who had fortifications and slave barracoons on nearby Grand Terre. Today, island roads are redolent with reminders, like the quintessential souvenir shop decorated with cutout cutthroats amidst the floats and fishbait and named Nez Coupé for the Genoan pirate Louis Chighizola, who lost his nose in a knife fight. In the peaceful old cemetery, the remains of Chighizolas, Rigauds, and other early settlers repose beneath inscriptions on marble in French: *"Ici repose la dépouille mortelle."*

Grand Isle hosted early agricultural experiments with sugarcane plantations under the Spanish regime of the late 1700s, then cucumber farms whose profitable produce could usually beat crops from other areas to market due to the island's tropical clime, but the salt bath from gulf breezes and the sandy soil proved less than hospitable. The seafood industry began early here as well, with Chinese immigrants, in the days before refrigeration, drying brine-bathed shrimp in the sun on raised platforms for export in barrels. Blue-painted luggers with three-cornered sails stained red with tan bark carried bell-shaped bamboo baskets piled high with shrimp, crabs, or fish and covered with Spanish moss.

When Martha R. Field, one of New Orleans' first female journalists, wrote travel columns for the late nineteenth-century *Daily Picayune*, she vividly described the Grand Isle fisheries industry in 1892, when the population was only about 550. According

to Field, island residents shipped sixteen thousand alligator hides to New Orleans merchants annually and tons of catfish weekly to western markets, "where they are sold as tenderloin of trout." Locals built large turtle pens and raised diamond-backed terrapins by the thousands for export, and semi-weekly mail boats returning from the island in winter were loaded with 1,200 brace of birds, ducks, and even deer. From nearby Last Island, she described the bird hunters' shocking booty:

> gulls and seabirds worth thirty-five cents apiece to garnish ball gowns or bonnets, pelicans killed for their pouches of which purses and tobacco bags are made and for the snow-white down on their breasts of which powder puffs are made and for the bones of their strong wings of which pipe stems are made; white cranes killed by the million for the aigrettes that grow between their shoulders; fans are sometimes made of the blue cranes wings, but the cruelest slaughter of all seems to be that of the aigrettes and the laughing gulls.

She also visited the "Chinese lake-dwellers in rush-thatched huts built over the gray lagoons, the yellow-skinned coolies plying their trade of shrimp drying, worshipping the joss, and eating their rice with sharp-pointed sticks of ivory and ebony, in bamboo hats," shipping $20,000 worth of dried fish and shrimp to China every year. Here they "danced the shrimp," shuffling around the sun-drying seafood with wrapped feet to separate the heads and shells while singing or chanting.

As late as the 1930s, Grand Isle still harbored free-roaming herds of wild cattle; there were orange groves and colorful oleanders, outside beehive ovens for baking bread, cisterns to catch fresh water, outhouses, and family meals cooked over fires of driftwood gathered along the beaches. The descendants of Creole settlers continued to speak their native French, although misguided efforts in public

Grand Isle cemetery, with epitaphs in French

Dense oak thickets of Grand Isle's bay harbor

Coast of Port Fourchon

Gulf waters provide excellent deep-sea fishing at Grand Isle.

schools had already begun to punish their children for doing so. In 1948, Humble Oil struck pay dirt with one of the world's first offshore drilling platforms. Today the island relies on fishing (both sport and commercial) and tourism, with cottages raised on piers whose seasonal occupants swell the normal population of two thousand to ten times that in summer and during the popular fishing rodeos, when the fishing boats return to port flying flags indicating the type of catch on board. In addition to a relaxed lifestyle cherished by residents and visitors alike, Grand Isle offers excellent birding, crabbing and shrimping, oystering, a beautiful butterfly dome at the Port Commission, a 140-acre state park on the beach with camping facilities and an observation tower, and world-class fishing in the Gulf waters and inland bays.

LA 1 is the bustling main street on this little island where there are more boats than cars. Before the shell road and bridge over Caminada Pass were completed in 1931, visitors arrived via a supply boat from the mainland, and not everyone was excited by the concrete connection. One early account de-

Boats fly flags indicating the catch onboard: here dolphin, swordfish, and tuna.

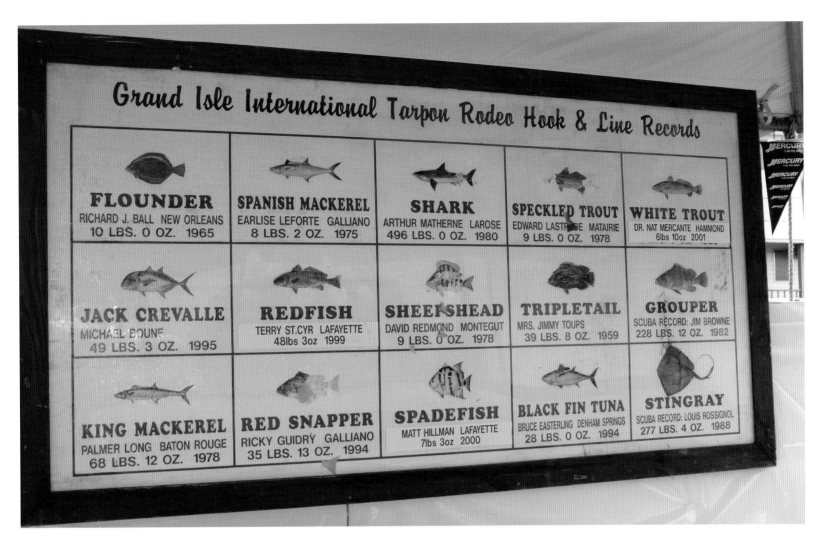

Grand Isle International Tarpon Rodeo Hook & Line Records

FLOUNDER	SPANISH MACKEREL	SHARK	SPECKLED TROUT	WHITE TROUT
RICHARD J. BALL NEW ORLEANS	EARLISE LEFORTE GALLIANO	ARTHUR MATHERNE LAROSE	EDWARD LASTRADE MATAIRIE	DR. NAT MERCANTE HAMMOND
10 LBS. 0 OZ. 1965	8 LBS. 2 OZ. 1975	496 LBS. 0 OZ. 1980	9 LBS. 0 OZ. 1978	6lbs 10oz 2001
JACK CREVALLE	REDFISH	SHEEPSHEAD	TRIPLETAIL	GROUPER
MICHAEL BOUNE	TERRY ST.CYR LAFAYETTE	DAVID REDMOND MONTEGUT	MRS. JIMMY TOUPS	SCUBA RECORD: JIM BROWNE
49 LBS. 3 OZ. 1995	48lbs 3oz 1999	9 LBS. 0 OZ. 1978	39 LBS. 8 OZ. 1959	228 LBS. 12 OZ. 1982
KING MACKEREL	RED SNAPPER	SPADEFISH	BLACK FIN TUNA	STINGRAY
PALMER LONG BATON ROUGE	RICKY GUIDRY GALLIANO	MATT HILLMAN LAFAYETTE	BRUCE EASTERLING DENHAM SPRINGS	SCUBA RECORD: LOUIS ROSSIGNOL
68 LBS. 12 OZ. 1978	35 LBS. 13 OZ. 1994	7lbs 3oz 2000	28 LBS. 0 OZ. 1994	277 LBS. 4 OZ. 1988

scribed the majority of islanders as "to progress oblivious, still a world apart . . . with the characteristic passivity of their predecessors who had witnessed the introduction and demise of plantations, resorts and other speculations on Grand Isle." Life was languid on Grand Isle, new things surged and ebbed like the tide without leaving much lasting impression, and islanders liked it that way. As the old accounts said, "Everyone worked, but easily."

In the antebellum years, plantation families spent entire summers on Louisiana's coastal islands for saltwater bathing and to escape the deadly yellow fever epidemics spread by mosquitoes across the mainland. Gentlemen oftentimes left wives and children on the coast as they returned for the workweek in New Orleans or on the sugar plantations. The Victorian ritual of bathing included bathhouses, gauze veils, two-piece bathing costumes of wool with ankle-length bloomers and even gloves to preserve delicate feminine modesty, and nowhere is a better picture drawn of this than in Kate Chopin's aptly titled Grand Isle novel *The Awakening*. One swanky beach hotel even provided a private bathhouse connected to each suite of rooms so that the ladies could step into the water for a refreshing bath "unseen by ogling masculine eyes."

Said Martha Reid in the late 1800s:

> In natural advantages, in situation, surf, climate, accessibility, forests, soil and immunity from dangerous storms, Grand Isle is, as the French would say, the bouquet of all the group of coastal islands. It has every qualification for an ideal winter resort, and is now one of the healthiest summer watering places in the world. Marvelous cures of nervous prostration,

Gentle waves wash Grand Isle beach.

paralysis, anemia, rheumatism and malaria have been made there. Only this month a gentleman severely paralyzed was taken to the island on a stretcher. He was carried to the beach and given surf baths. At the end of a week he could sit up, and at the end of three weeks he walked on board the boat and left the island a well man.

If the miraculous medical cures were exaggerations, the professed immunity from dangerous storms was downright wishful thinking, although Grand Isle has indeed been luckier than other coastal islands like Isle Dernière, which was wiped out in August 1856 with enormous loss of life. Afterwards it was called "the island of the curse of God, where flowers bloom not, where no clean nor honest life is, and where even the bird hunters camp with fear and trembling, because of the ghosts of those who were drowned there during the storm of '56."

Bayou Lafourche plantation owner Col. W. W. Pugh, who lost a baby daughter, Loula, in the storm, wrote of the hurricane: "When I think of its violence, I do not wonder that so many persons perished, but am rather surprised that any were saved." With horror still palpable years later, he recalled when the storm hit, as the bay waters were blown over the narrow island and into the gulf:

> Now the struggle for life commenced and horror was painted on every face, no one exposed could withstand the force of the waves, and all who were caught without shelter or something to hold onto fell victims to the merciless waters. Some floated off to unknown parts on pieces of timber, several took passage on a billiard table, two colored boys found safety in a bake oven . . . When morning came at last, a scene of great desolation presented itself. There was not a house left standing . . . and the bodies of the drowned could be seen in every direction, arrested by the prairie grass and low shrubs.

Just as hard hit by successive hurricanes, Grand

Fishing at the Fourchon

A thunderstorm sweeps across the marshes at Fourchon.

Surf fishing on a chilly day at Grand Isle

Observation tower overlooks the beach at Grand Isle.

The Port Commission butterfly dome

Isle survives because of its residents' determination and also because of the hardiness of the live oaks shading the Bayou Rigaud side of the island, providing shelter amidst lush undergrowth. There were massive oaks along much of the coast in the early days, growing in cheniers (oak groves), their roots holding soil together and helping cleanse the waters, their canopies cutting the wind and giving lifesaving shade. Blown into leaning postures by the blustery winds, the oaks of Grand Isle were seen by nineteenth-century writer Lafcadio Hearn as "fleeing women with streaming garments and windblown hair, bowing grievously and thrusting out arms desperately northward to save themselves from falling." Many have maintained that the oaks have repeatedly saved Grand Isle.

22

Chênière Caminada

Lafcadio Hearn observed the constant strife and state of flux along the Louisiana coastline as the Mississippi River shifted deltas over the ages: "Forever the yellow Mississippi strives to build, forever the sea struggles to destroy—and amid their eternal strife the islands and the promontories change shape more slowly but not less fantastically than the clouds of heaven."

They call it a land apart, south of The South, a place where the past isn't the past at all but the present. Local newspaperman John DeSantis says that here "the past and present are wrapped so comfortably in each other's arms that it's hard to see where one ends and the other begins."

In all truthfulness, Louisiana's bayou country is indeed a land like no other. If you can even call it land, these *prairies tremblants* and *amblants*, in this area called *flotants*, forever shifting, trembling, quavering and moving like mirages. Author Harnett Kane wrote that no other part of the coast was such a battlefield of elements all working for change, upbuilding, disintegrating, wearing, scouring, depositing. He called lower Louisiana a place unable to make up its mind whether to be earth or water, and so belonging wholeheartedly to neither element.

LA 1 lies just slightly above sea level here, the marsh grass and inland waters lapping at its roadbed along this stretch, the power poles braced to withstand hurricane winds and the cemetery guarded by its lone dead tree, killed by saltwater surge. Originally inhabited by Chitimacha Indians, Chênière Caminada became a refuge for many of Lafitte's pirates.

Power poles braced to withstand hurricane winds along lower LA 1

24

HURRICANE OF 1893

The residents of this little fishing community made the mistake of cutting many of the native oaks to plant orange groves and vineyards and also to build and heat houses. In 1893, a late-season fast-moving hurricane smashed the sleeping *chênière* with 125-mile-an-hour winds and waters surging twenty or thirty feet deep. With few trees for protection, the death toll included more than half the 1,500 inhabitants. According to some accounts, grieving survivors hastily buried the dead with their hands or sticks because the waves had carried off all the shovels and the materials to make coffins. In the first four days after the storm, Father Grimeaux, a Catholic priest, assisted with 460 burials. On the LA 1 roadside, the austere Chênière Caminada Cemetery contains many of the victims in mass graves.

Of hundreds of family homes, only a dozen or two were left, and hardly a boat was still seaworthy. The Chênière church bell—said to have been cast from nineteenth-century pirate silver and the fam-

ily plate of the local pastor—tolled throughout the night of the storm. Only when the tower was cast into the raging waters did the bell's clangor cease. Miraculously, it was recovered after the waters subsided and taken off the island; when another church obtained permission to use it, the bell mysteriously disappeared (most versions of the story have it buried in a graveyard) until it could be used "to ring again for Baratarians" at Our Lady of the Isle Church at Grand Isle, where it hangs today.

Leeville

From Leeville near the Gulf of Mexico northward to Donaldsonville, LA 1 closely parallels Bayou Lafourche, long the center of transportation and community life, and still lined with shrimp trawlers with their graceful fluttering butterfly nets, oyster luggers, and all manner of other boats bespeaking a thriving fisheries industry. The small Acadian homesteads that once lined the bayou were so close in proximity that this was called the longest street in the world, where news called out of the window or over the *pieux* picket fence could travel from house to house down the bayou faster than it could be delivered by automobile. Supplies and mail were transported by boat along the bayou, and—in certain locales—so were the schoolchildren.

Originally named Orange City because of all the groves of citrus trees, Leeville took in many refugees from the Chênière Caminada hurricane of 1893, the year the town was officially founded and renamed for Pierre Charles Lee. But in 1915 the 140-mph winds of yet another hurricane swept in waters up to twenty feet deep and destroyed ninety-nine of Leeville's one hundred buildings, sending many of its surviving residents to seek new homes farther north along the bayou.

Early settlers provided citrus and seafood for the New Orleans French Market, but energy exploration transformed life along the bayou beginning in the 1930s, with the first oilfield discovery in Leeville. In 1938, Leeville became Lafourche Parish's oil pro-

Port Fourchon

ducing capital with 297 producing wells, and Lower Lafourche was transformed into a "Wild West boomtown" with outsiders attracted by the profitable work. Once the first out-of-sight offshore rig went up off the coast of Morgan City, the area also saw the birth of local spin-off industries catering to the oil business—shipbuilding, manufacturing drilling equipment, repairs, supplies.

At Leeville, Bayou Lafourche widens and heads off through the marsh to reach the Gulf at what is called the Fourchon, bustling with boat traffic. Besides the bayou transportation, a large amount of the traffic is now also along LA 1, going to Louisiana's southernmost port, "the Gulf's Energy Connection" at busy Port Fourchon. Some ten thousand vehicles including one thousand big trucks a day transport equipment and support personnel for the offshore platforms producing a sizable percentage of the na-

tion's oil and gas. Within forty miles, there are over six hundred platforms, all serviced by supply boats and tugboats operating out of Port Fourchon, so the port's significance to the entire nation's energy infrastructure is unparalleled. Within Louisiana alone, the energy industry provides more than 300,000 jobs and has a $70 billion annual impact.

Louisiana Offshore Oil Port (LOOP), the first offshore oil terminal in the United States, is southeast of Port Fourchon in the Gulf, where it offloads oil from supertankers into pipelines connected to more than 50 percent of the nation's refining capacity, and booster pumps convey crude oil from LOOP to underground salt-dome storage areas in Galliano along LA 1. Each day, LOOP transports over a million barrels of foreign oil and a third that much domestic crude from the Gulf's outer continental shelf. The area is crucial to the country's oil supply as well

Shrimp boats on Bayou Lafourche

as to its pocketbook; the government collects an annual $5 billion in oil and gas revenues and royalties from Louisiana's offshore drilling.

But look at the Leeville Cemetery, which began in 1905 during a month-long yellow fever epidemic, and the constant struggle of this area to stay afloat becomes clear. In an effort to keep more graves from washing away, the cemetery along the roadside has been completely cemented over—tombs, ground, and all. Like the cemetery, LA 1 along here is often

completely underwater during even minor tropical storms, much less hurricanes. Surrounded by open water that used to be marsh, it is now broken only by lifeless leafless trees killed by saltwater intrusion from storm surges that are coming farther and farther inland each year as more of the coastline erodes. Because low-lying, two-lane LA 1 and the drawbridge at Leeville, raised dozens of times a day for heavy boat traffic, have traditionally been the only land-based transportation route to Port Fourchon as well

28

as the only hurricane evacuation route for Grand Isle residents, much of Lower Lafourche, and thousands of offshore oil workers, a new raised roadway and a high fixed bridge branch off here to provide much-needed improved access—escape.

The eyes of the world focused on this area when the Deepwater Horizon drilling rig exploded and sank in the spring of 2010, releasing a catastrophic oil spill into gulf waters and reminding that Louisiana's offshore oil industry, while providing energy resources and much-needed jobs, is at best a mixed blessing.

Concrete keeps floodwaters from washing away Leeville Cemetery.

The old Leeville Bridge, long an impediment to hasty LA 1 traffic flow since cars had to give way to boats, has been replaced with a new higher fixed span crossing Bayou Lafourche.

Beginning construction of high fixed bridge over Bayou Lafourche

Golden Meadow

Golden Meadow was probably named for the vast fields of golden wildflowers early settlers found growing there. Today, goldenrod brightens wide expanses of ground, and in the swamplands there are thousands of wild Louisiana iris (the French *fleur-de-lis* and Louisiana's state flower), flowering vines, and other exotic and fascinating plantlife proliferating jungle-like in this subtropical climate.

Many of the survivors of the coastal island hurricanes moved up the bayou to settle small communities they hoped would be safer, but even in Golden Meadow the 1915 hurricane left seaweed fourteen feet up a cypress tree. Floodgates were installed, with locks at Golden Meadow and Larose, to shut off Bayou Lafourche and keep the storm surge out during hurricanes, which protects some areas but diverts the flooding into the Intracoastal and Houma Navigation Canal instead, thereby endangering other areas. The locks are part of the levee system designed to protect Lower Lafourche, although Hurricane Katrina came close to topping the levees in 2005. As water comes farther and farther inland and Louisiana's coast erodes, many heliports and oilfield supply and support operations are moving from the coast farther north along the bayou to prevent work stoppages throughout hurricane season.

In Golden Meadow, LA 1 travels directly beside Bayou Lafourche, separated only by a small seawall. There are shrimp boats, shrimp sheds, and all sorts of shrimp processing plants along this stretch, and the colorful blessing of the fleet ceremony was introduced here in 1916, all in French, of course. Hurricanes Katrina and Rita, the first and third costliest storms in U.S. history, caused more than $2 billion damage to the shrimp industry in 2005, dropping shrimp trawl licenses 50 percent in 2006 in Louisiana alone. Yet the storms somehow produced conditions (perhaps nutrients that should have enriched

The *Little Binny* approaches the locks at Golden Meadow.

the land ending up in the gulf waters instead) resulting in a record catch in 2006 of nearly sixty-nine thousand metric tons of shrimp, 10 percent more than season averages from the four years prior to the hurricanes, and the shrimper advocacy group Wild American Shrimp noted that the catch included shrimp larger in size and full of flavor.

Only a small seawall separates LA 1 from Bayou Lafourche at Golden Meadow.

Le Petit Caporal

Golden Meadow's town icon is *Le Petit Caporal*, a shrimp boat built in 1854 and named for the diminutive Napoleon Bonaparte. Used for commercial fishing, it first operated under sail and then became the earliest motorized vessel in the area when Leon Theriot, Sr., installed a 3 hp tractor motor in 1902. His eight sons—Henry, Davis, Victor, Paris, Fedalise, Leopold, Leon, Jr., and Leo—worked the *Caporal*, the oldest vessel on record. Now the *Caporal* is on permanent display in dry dock and usually flanked by big modern fishing boats with their high-tech gear on the bayou, providing a study in shrimping industry improvements and innovations over the years. This oldest shrimp boat in Golden Meadow was slightly damaged by Hurricane Betsy in September 1965, when winds clocked at 150 mph did $100 million in damage to Lower Lafourche, demolished 4,500 homes, left only 5 percent of the buildings still standing at Grand Isle, and overturned the Lockport water tower, spilling 55,000 gallons of water over the town. In September 2008, Hurricane Gustav severely damaged the *Caporal*.

Galliano and Cut Off

These communities also served as refuges for survivors and relocated houses of the Chênière Caminada hurricane of October 1893. Five months before the devastating storm, Nicholas Curole built a simple wood frame raised Creole cottage at Caminadaville for his bride Celina Gaspard, only to have it heavily damaged by wind and storm surge. The following year, the house was relocated, rebuilt, and no doubt whitewashed in the section along LA 1 called Cote Blanche (White Coast) for the multitude of little white houses erected by the storm refugees. It stands today, according to its historic marker, as a symbol of the valiant struggle of the hurricane survivors. Local writer/moviemaker Glen Pitre tells the story of one hurricane survivor who, en route up the bayou in the rescue boat, spotted his own house listing along the bank where it had been blown some eight or nine miles upstream by the winds; he jumped overboard, swam ashore and moved right in.

Before the Curole House and several hundred Caminada storm survivors moved here, many of the homes along this stretch of the bayou, housing Indians as well as early pioneering families were constructed of upright cypress posts and had dirt floors.

Curole House

The walls were filled with mud and moss insulation called *bousillage*, and the house, which was roofed with palmetto thatching, typically had a chimney made of twigs filled with mud and moss as well.

Creoles, Germans, Italians, and Cajuns—descendants of Acadian exiles—populated the communities. Acadians, pushed out of Nova Scotia by the British in the Grand Dérangement of 1755, moved into the area in the latter half of the eighteenth century and steadily expanded down the bayou as the hurricane survivors of coastal communities moved steadily up stream. The transplanted Canadians and their descendants adapted their traditional way of life to the Louisiana climate, building tiny raised houses with Creole improvements like cross-ventilation, shady galleries, and cypress shingles instead of thatch roofing; they also forsook their cold-weather crops (wheat, flax, turnips, apples) from their homeland for those more suitable to a hot humid environment, and replaced their customary woolen dress with cool homespun cotonade. By 1788, it was estimated that Acadians constituted over 60 percent of the total population of the Lafourche District.

Settlement in Galliano began as early as the 1830s with the arrival of the families of Zenon Cheramie and Onézime Hebert (surnames still prominent in the bayou country today). The community was probably called Cote Cheramie until renamed for prosperous Italian immigrant Salvador Galliano, who in the 1860s had four hundred acres of rice and orange groves.

Dale Rogers' reminiscences explain that Cut Off's name was derived from a short-cut canal intended to connect it to New Orleans through Lake Salvador. Construction begun in 1900 with six mules dragging a heavy piece of wood, over and over again, to scrape away the ground to the desired depth. Groceries were delivered weekly by flatboat or barge, and the packet merchant went house to house on foot carrying his merchandise on his back. The Cut Off store was built in 1900, but most residents shopped for supplies every couple of months,

Grand Isle residents twice a year.

The folks along this stretch of the bayou sure knew how to pass a good time. Turn-of-the-century dances enlivened every Saturday night at rotating farmsteads. Participants moved furniture out to make way for the dancers, whose horses were tied to the picket fence or the chinaberry tree in the host's yard. The children were put to bed early for the *fais do-do*, and musicians like William Pitre played violin for $1.50 a night, all night. Dance halls came into popularity around 1915, with music by local musicians and even visiting groups like The Ball of Sweets from New Orleans at the Baljour Dance Hall, or the Baby Guidry hall, or Joe Perrin's Place in Golden Meadow, where the guests arrived by 3 hp boats. In Lockport during the 1930s, Jitney Dances took place on Sunday nights at the pavilion on Main Street, with gents paying five cents to dance with a lady while her mother "sat on the sidelines keeping a watchful eye."

Facility for letting the good times roll must be hereditary, for there still are some hot nightspots in the area, like PJ's Fed Pond in Golden Meadow, where Cajun dancing enlivens sultry Saturday nights. Other famous dance halls have long been abandoned, like the Hubba-Hubba and the enormous unpainted Lee Brothers dancehall, which drew crowds from

"Turn-of-the-century dances enlivened every Saturday night at rotating farmsteads."

Long-popular Lee Brothers dancehall was used as a setting in *The Home Front*.

as far up the bayou as Raceland in the 1930s and 1940s. Located right along LA 1 at bayou's edge, Glen Pitre used it in the World War II-era movie *The Scoundrel's Wife* (released on DVD as *The Home Front*), which explores rumors that local collaborators smuggled illegal immigrants and supplied diesel to German U-boats torpedoing Gulf shipping at a time when several German prisoner-of-war camps existed in southwest Louisiana. The stunning IMAX film *Hurricane on the Bayou* is Pitre's latest production as writer and co-director.

Joseph Felicien Larose, early druggist who arranged for Larose to have its first post office, gave the town its name. Late 1800s New Orleans travel writer Martha R. Field called this area a country of fabulous riches, crowded population, and a most charming aspect, saying: "Bayou Lafourche is almost as populously settled as St. Charles Avenue. Not an acre goes to waste; not an arpent lies idle."

The 150-foot-wide, heavily trafficked Intracoastal Canal, considered a vital link in the national inland east-west canal system, crosses Bayou Lafourche at the locks. The boat captains' skill makes squeezing some larger vessels through the very nar-

row lock opening look easier than it is. Watching the boat parade is one of the highlights of driving LA 1 along Bayou Lafourche, where dozens of towering lift bridges and drawbridges open to allow the trawlers, luggers, and other crafts to pass as auto traffic comes to a halt.

In the Grand Bois community live a large number of Houma Indians, who have traditionally made their living off the land, fishing, trapping, hunting, and farming. Today many work in the oilfield industries as well. Their Powwows provide good opportunities to view native Indian dress as well as intricate crafts and dances as tribal members struggle to preserve their cultural identity. Larose also hosts an annual Cajun Heritage Festival, where some of the most popular and incredibly beautiful exhibits and competitions feature traditional Cajun duck decoy woodcarvings.

This is also an ideal area to begin watching for big beautiful bald eagles fishing along the bayou,

Junction of the Intracoastal Canal and Bayou Lafourche at Larose

swooping down to catch a fish or snake in their talons. America's national bird made an encouraging comeback since pesticide contamination placed it on the endangered species list, and coastal Louisiana now hosts hundreds of them along the freshwater swamps and brackish marshes. Eagle nests, weighing upwards of one hundred pounds, are not hard to spot atop tall sturdy cypress trees or sometimes even power poles.

The Larose bridge is raised for tug passage along the Intracoastal Canal.

Lockport

In 1790, the Spanish crown awarded the first land grant of Lockport property, but the completion of the Company Canal connecting Bayou Lafourche with markets in New Orleans across Lake Salvador in 1847 made this watery crossroads the commercial center of central Lafourche at that time. Land was donated to the Barataria and Lafourche Canal Company by the landowner whose barge line, which transported harvested sugarcane, needed a more direct route not necessitating a laborious transfer of the cargo to steamships along the Mississippi River. When the locks were built in 1850, the settlement got its name, though it was not incorporated until 1899. Parts of these picturesque brick locks were washed away in the crevasse of 1917.

The first school in Lockport was constructed from a wooden barge, an old produce boat, with a mud chimney; it accommodated up to twenty-five students. The school ferry was hand-pulled across Bayou Lafourche using a winch. The wire cable that stretched across the bayou had to be lowered if a tugboat rounded the bend.

Pierre Joseph Claudet built the historic Bouverans Plantation House around 1860 and named it for his native village in France. Today, it remains in the same family, its white picket fences and grounds in immaculate condition.

The bayou was the fastest means of transportation. First flatboats delivered goods and produce, and then shallow-draft steamboats with rear pad-

Historic brick locks gave the community of Lockport its name.

Bouverans Plantation House

interests. Today it operates thirteen shipyards in South Louisiana and Texas, welding together every sort of vessel, including Coast Guard cutters. Since the oil boom of the 1930s, other innovative bayou boat builders like Edison Chouest Offshore have provided crewboats and workboats, supply boats and high-tech vessels for use throughout the world in oilfield service and supply.

Even in the early days, Lockport was noted as a center of boat building, and craftsmen, who often spoke

dlewheels—due to the narrowness of the bayous—made regular runs with passengers and freight. Showboats brought a floating touch of culture to the bayou with travelling theatrical productions and operas and a zoo boat that must have been reminiscent of old Noah's Ark. Because roadways were so bad, the earliest cars were rendered nearly useless, and life centered around boats and bayous into the twentieth century, with boys growing up aboard the family shrimpers and taking charge of their own boats as young teens.

It was only natural that boat building became one of the major occupations in Lockport. Louisiana, after all, has more shipbuilding establishments than any other state to provide not only the means of transport for goods and passengers, but also to satisfy the needs of its fisheries industries and the huge offshore oil industry. Lockport is home to the Bollinger Shipyard founded in 1946 to provide full repair and construction services for marine and oil

only French, handcrafted a wonderful variety of vessels. The cypress *pirogue* so well suited for narrow bayous was adapted from the Indian dugouts. Small flatboats propelled by sail or oars and pushpoles provided the early utility transport for passengers, produce, and cargo. Sail-powered fishing vessels called *canots* could either travel with the wind or be towed by mules or men on towpaths pulling *la cordelle*. The crews could seine in the bays for shrimp, but could not venture too far from shore. It was in 1917 when the modern shrimp trawl was introduced, and its use along with gasoline engines, refrigeration, and improved navigation aids led to boom years in the commercial shrimping industry.

The Center for Traditional Louisiana Boat Building at Nicholls State University in nearby Thibodaux has ambitious plans to display its large collection of wooden boats, antique photographs, and artifacts in the old Ford building, next to the Lafourche Heri-

The Lockport Company Canal Bridge towers above the abandoned *Doris Marie*.

tage Museum in Lockport by the intersection of the Company Canal with Bayou Lafourche. The collection includes a three hundred-year-old bald cypress Indian dugout canoe among dozens of other vessels, and at times visitors may actually see boat building on site.

Nearby, the nice little bayouside park on Canal St., longtime resting place of the vintage vessel *Doris Marie*, marks the southern terminus of the annual Bayou Lafourche canoe trip sponsored by the Barrataria-Terrebonne National Estuary Program. The event permits dozens of paddlers from around the country to get up close and personal with the waterway for fifty-two miles, from its beginnings at Donaldsonville on the Mississippi River to Lockport. Along the way, they are serenaded by accordions, stuffed with seafood, and welcomed with the *joie de vivre* for which this section is famous. The big boat traffic is too heavy below Lockport for the canoes to proceed safely further south.

Doris Marie

Paddle Lafourche participants traverse fifty-two miles of upper bayou every spring.

Mathews and Raceland

From the black gold of the oil boom to the white gold of the sugar bowl region, the fertile lands LA 1 traverses as it follows Bayou Lafourche up from the coast have seen many a fortune made and many a fortune lost to the vagaries of hurricanes, early frosts, market fluctuations, war, flooding, diseases, and all the other unpredictable factors that make planting as much of a gamble as oil production. Yet the lush lands along the bayou had been enriched over the centuries by nutrient-laden floodwaters, and the mild climate and plentiful rainfall proved perfect for the production of sugarcane, which under ideal conditions can grow more than an inch a day in the summer to reach a height of twelve feet or more. The navigable canals and bayous and the mighty Mississippi provided the means of moving the harvest to market, and before the Civil War, labor was plentiful and cheap on the sugar plantations.

Sugarcane had an enormous impact on land development and settlement along Bayou Lafourche, mostly north of the Intracoastal Canal. Cane operations required immense acreages and a huge labor force. The *petit habitations*, the small farms of the early Acadian exiles and other immigrants, were engulfed by larger plantations after the influx of American planters beginning in the 1820s and '30s, and the small farmers were pushed back away from the rich bayoulands into the swampy *brulés*. At the same time, slave laborers were introduced for the first time in appreciable numbers. The introduction of hardy, disease-resistant ribbon cane, well suited to the south Louisiana climate, combined with favorable tariffs

Harvesting sugarcane

Bayou Lafourche is flanked by LA 1 and LA 308.

A cropduster swoops low over a field of sugarcane.

White Gold Sugar was produced on Georgia Plantation in Mathews.

and Etienne de Boré's improved granulation methods to make sugarcane a more profitable crop in this region than indigo or cotton. By 1846, the Bayou Lafourche area had nearly one hundred sugar mills, many of them steam-powered, greatly increasing the output of the small early animal-powered mills.

Life centered around the seasons of the sugarcane crop: Plowing began in January, followed by planting of the seed cane in furrows, cultivating of the fields with hoes through the hot months, cutting wood for fuel and barrels, and repairing mill machinery. The seasonal cycle culminated with the late fall harvest and grinding season, when work was frantic and nonstop around the clock as the cane was cut with big two-foot cane knives in the fields and hauled to the mill in carts drawn by the big "sugar mules" or, later, dummy trains. In the sugarhouse, the sugar was extracted from the cane in a five-step process—grinding the cane to extract the juice, purifying the juice, evaporating the juice into a viscous syrup, granulating the syrup into sugar crystals, and separating the molasses from the crystals. The cane passed through a series of cast-iron kettles, gradu-

ated in size, called the kettle train, and, at the end of the process, the molasses was separated out into barrels and the sugar eventually packed into huge wooden hogsheads for shipment, often by steamboat, to New Orleans and markets on the East Coast or in the West.

The Mathews family had a big sugarcane operation on their Georgia Plantation, and they gave that little settlement its name. Today, one of the most interesting stops in town is the venerable Adams Fruit Stand, selling everything from fresh honey and vegetables to turtle and alligator meat, live worms and cast nets, poboys and hunting licenses. The mini-museum inside exhibits a twelve-foot alligator, an albino nutria, a variety of trapping equipment and some rather eye-catching arrangements focusing on frog legs.

Mathews runs right into the town of Raceland, which was named for its nineteenth-century horse racing tracks, but it was the big Godchaux Sugar Mill, begun in Raceland in 1891, that assured the town's success. In the early years, Raceland was overshadowed by neighboring Bowie, a bustling sawmill town that housed the large workforce of the Bowie Lumber Company's Cypress King Mill until the whole town burned down in 1917.

Today there are only two functional sugar mills

Sunset at a sugar mill

in Lafourche Parish, but Raceland Raw Sugars and Lafourche Sugars Corporation process nearly two million tons of sugar a year—some of which is brought in from other parishes. In 2006, there were just over twenty-five thousand acres of cane harvested in Lafourche, reflecting a decrease in production and lands planted with cane. Just as the sugar planters elbowed out the small subsistence farmers along the bayou, new modern subdivisions are pushing the planters out of the higher land to construct homes in areas safer from flooding, and land use patterns are in flux again. But don't count King Sugar out. It is still Louisiana's leading plant commodity, produced on a half-million acres in twenty-three parishes. Each acre yields an average of forty tons of cane, and each ton of cane makes around two hundred pounds of sugar. Louisiana produces about 20 percent of the sugar grown in the United States.

Raceland Raw Sugars stands in the midst of canefields.

Lafourche Crossing

At the time of the Civil War, the rich farmlands along Bayou Lafourche were considered the breadbasket of Louisiana, producing not only sugar, but also corn, rice, cotton, and other agricultural staples. By 1862, the area was also a buffer zone between Yankee soldiers determined to ward off any contemplated attacks on Union-held New Orleans, and Confederates determined to halt Yankee movement westward.

Control of the waterways in the area was vitally important, but so was control of the railroad completed in the 1850s to connect the Lafourche district with New Orleans. Construction gangs battled floods, yellow fever epidemics, financial difficulties, swamps, marshes, and trembling prairies, not to mention bayous requiring bridge crossings. The track of the New Orleans, Opelousas, and Great Western Railroad crossed Bayou Lafourche four miles south of Thibodaux at Lafourche Crossing. In the summer of 1863, this became the site of the only major battle in Lafourche Parish.

Several companies of Confederate soldiers were raised from the Lafourche district, but sentiments in the area were mixed regarding Louisiana's secession from the Union in January 1861; the issue of slavery concerned only the largest landholders, like Franklin Pugh who heard the news and recorded in his diary, "All honour to the men who had the courage to take this first step to prosperity which will be as permanent as earthly things may be." But in Thibodaux, Father Charles Menard, well-loved priest who served parish Roman Catholics for fifty-three years, feared the church bells pealing to announce the secession were sounding the country's death knell.

The early skirmishes and forays by rail and afoot in the area were not without lighter moments, as noted in the wonderfully detailed account of the battle in *Touched By War* by Nicholls University professor Christopher Pena (the ensuing quotes from soldiers are all drawn from this book). In early summer 1862, Maj. Charles Dillingham of the 8th Vermont marched his command past the young ladies' seminary at Mount Carmel Academy in Thibodaux and noted the windows filled with curious young faces seeking a glimpse of the awful Yankee invaders. "Being noted for gallantry toward the fair sex," he called a halt and had his band serenade the students, followed by three cheers for the "sweet girl graduates," and three more for the dear old flag. (When the Sisters of Mount Carmel sold the convent building in 1965 and it was torn down to make way for a modern motel, a deal was struck to preserve the convent's dainty little Victorian cupola, which now sits atop the motel roof as if blown in by hurricane winds from another century.)

The Union soldiers deployed to this unfamiliar part of the country were both amazed at the

The Victorian cupola from nineteenth-century Mount Carmel convent tops a modern motel.

Railroad bridge at Lafourche Crossing

lush loveliness of the landscape and horrified at the dangers lurking in its swamps. A Union corporal from Massachusetts found the area

> perfectly charming, the sweetest of regions, with the sweetest of air. Seldom does an army march under circumstances so delightful . . . We shall carry home a much more favorable impression as to the resources and civilization of this State than we should have had if we had not passed through this country of the La Fourche.

A private from Vermont wrote in horror of the alligators and snakes "too numerous to mention" and above all the

> mosquetoes [*sic*] . . . all of them large enough to climb a tree and bark, and what was worse, bite through a thick woolen blanket and pair of pants. The story of the man who crawled under a kettle to

escape a swarm of mosquetoes [*sic*], how they smelled his blood and lighting upon it drove their bills through while he buried himself heading them down inside, untill at last, they flew away taking the kettle with them, was looked upon more leniently than it had been previous.

Yet as the fighting commenced, the boys of both sides had little time to be concerned with the scenery or the swamp creatures. As one young corporal from Connecticut wrote, "I have said that I wanted to be in a fight, but the Lord knows that I don't want to be in another one." Sentiments surely echoed on both sides of the battlefield.

The two-day battle at Lafourche Crossing on June 20–21, 1863, pitted approximately two hundred Confederates under Col. James P. Major, including some dashing cavalry regiments from Texas led by Col. Charles L. Pyron, against Federal forces numbering more than six hundred under command of Lt. Col. Albert Stickney.

Civil War re-enactors set up authentic encampment at E. D. White Historic Site.

Civil War re-enactors fire a cannon at Laurel Valley.

The first day Confederate forces liberated Union-held Thibodaux. Their wild cavalry charges so astonished the Federals that "they stayed not for compliments, but made good use of horse legs, mule legs, and legs generally, to cover the four mile road between Thibodaux and Lafourche Crossing in the shortest running time on record." The liberators were welcomed by the townsfolk, with cheering ladies waving and proffering baskets of "all kind of drinks and eatables."

From the captured Federal commissary and quartermaster stores, the Confederates gained badly needed Enfield rifles, but the gallant Texans, referred to by Gen. Richard Taylor as "hardy and brave and zealous, but lacking in discipline," also rather overzealously liberated too many barrels of "red eye," no doubt hampering their effectiveness for the second day of battle. They attacked like desperadoes, with wild rebel yells that one Yankee likened to "a mingling of Indian whoop and wolfhowl," and another said made his hair stand on end "like quills upon the fretful porcupine." Recorded one Connecticut private,

> The Confederates, full of whiskey and gunpower (as was ascertained by the examination of their canteens left on the battlefield in front of the Union Breastworks), which made them utterly regardless of life, came up to the very mouths of our cannon during the engagement, and placing their hands upon them, demanded their surrender. The audacious Confederates were either shot down or bayoneted where they stood.

A fierce storm blowing across Lafourche on June 21 rendered many of the Confederate guns inoperable, and with no way to dry their ammunition, the rainsoaked greycoats collected their casualties and abandoned the fray as night fell on June 22.

Thibodaux

"The charming little town of Thibodaux . . . is the best managed, the cleanest and neatest town in the state, laid out with the regularity of a chess board. The residences, modestly retiring from the public view, wear on their gables draperies of rose and honeysuckle vine. Mockingbirds sing in every tree," wrote Martha R. Field, travel writer for a New Orleans newspaper in the late 1800s. Thibodaux still prides itself on being a charming and clean community, even now that it is the bustling commercial center of the Lafourche district and a booming college town as well. Thibodaux celebrates Mardi Gras in a big way, and its long-established Firemen's Fair is one of the most popular festivals around.

Henry Schuyler Thibodaux received a Spanish land grant in 1794 from Gov. Francisco Luis Hector, baron de Carondelet, and began development of the settlement, which became an important trading post for the Lafourche country and was incor-

porated as a town in 1838. By 1840, there were five hundred residents receiving their mail twice a week from Donaldsonville via the bayou and bartering their sugar and molasses with the small steamers or Ohio River flatboats that descended the waterway loaded with corn, meat, potatoes, apples, whiskey, flour, and dry goods.

The town's muddy streets were lined with *banquettes* made of flatboat gunwales, and by 1847 a contract was let for a ferry across the bayou. The ferryman was required to keep a skiff for foot passengers and a substantial flatboat capable of crossing four horses at a time, and he had to be at the landing from daybreak to 9 p.m., sleep in the ferry house, maintain levees on both banks, and cross all comers within fifteen minutes or else pay a fine. Charges for crossings were set by the town at five cents per person, individual horse, or horned cattle, four cents for sheep and hogs, and forty or fifty cents for two-wheeled carriages. Licensed ministers and militia rode free of charge.

When Thibodaux constructed a power station to provide electricity, residents recalled the excitement when the streetlights were scheduled to be turned on. Florence Simoneaud and Mrs. Evangeline Torres reminisced, "Everyone stood at his front gate in the dark to witness the spectacle. How we all cheered and applauded when the street became visible for a few blocks down!" The two sisters also recalled the 1890s when their father ran a general merchandise store, and the family lived in a raised Creole cottage with surrounding fence, sleeping on moss mattresses under mosquito bars, cooking on wood stoves, drinking cistern water, boiling the laundry weekly in iron cauldrons, and lighting the home with kerosene and candles. Vividly they remembered the droves of cattle driven through the streets to the stockyard, saying, "Papa

would quickly shut the store's front doors when he saw the cattle coming. One of the town's citizens had been attacked and gored to death in such an invasion." And then there were the dirt roads, dusty in dry weather and well-nigh impassable with deep sticky mud in the rain. In fact, one horse-drawn funeral cortege had to disembark and roll the coffin along the sidewalk in a wheelbarrow.

Henry S. Thibodaux rose to fame as a Louisiana legislator who served as acting governor when the sitting governor died and Thibodaux, as president of the senate, was elevated to fill the position until the next election. But he would not be the only area resident to make good. Three Confederate generals called the area home. Gen. Braxton Bragg owned a plantation nearby. Leonidas Polk, first Episcopal Bishop of Louisiana, lived at Leighton Plantation and established St. John's Church in Thibodaux in 1843 as the first Episcopal church built west of the Mississippi. The Fighting Bishop of the Confederacy was killed at the Battle of Pine Mountain, and in the St. John's churchyard stands a memorial in his honor. Consecrated by Bishop Polk on Palm Sunday 1844, the church was abruptly closed from February 1864 through the duration of the Civil War when its rector, a native of Maryland, refused to pray for President Lincoln or take an oath of allegiance to the United States.

St. John's peaceful oak-shaded cemetery is also the resting place of Francis Tillou Nicholls, distinguished Confederate brigadier general, twice governor of Louisiana and chief justice of the Louisiana Supreme Court. Nicholls, in whose honor the growing local university was named, raised a company of infantry and led them in the Civil War.

He lost an arm and a foot in battle, so that when he announced his candidacy for governor of Louisiana in 1887, the nomination was made for "all that is left of Francis Tillou Nicholls." His grave commands attention in the St. John's cemetery, which is filled with historic markers, some tombs holding victims of the Isle Dernière hurricane and other catastrophes. Some are impressive, and some merely heartbreaking, like that of little Lewis Pugh Prescott, only son of L.D. Prescott and Mildred Pugh, atop whose tombstone leans a chubby marble cherub as if reading the inscription, "It is only a little grave, Just a little child that's dead, But much of light, of hope, of joy, lies buried with our angel boy." Periodic presentations called Grave Affairs raise funds for cemetery upkeep by allowing select historical figures like Bishop Polk and Governor Nicholls to rise from the tombs and tell their stories as evening falls.

Another significant church in Thibodaux is the Renaissance Romanesque St. Joseph Co-Cathedral, with elaborate ceiling frescoes, magnificent stained

Left: St. John's Episcopal Church
Above: Pensive cherub marks the tombstone of little Lewis Pugh Prescott in St. John's cemetery.

glass windows and a relic of St. Valerie, virgin martyr beheaded in Rome during the second-century persecutions of Christians. Sealed in a reliquary and shipped across the ocean, then up from New Orleans via Bayou Lafourche in 1818 aboard a steamboat, St. Valerie was welcomed to St. Joseph's in ceremonies attended by more than four thousand worshippers. When the cathedral caught fire in 1916 and could obviously not be saved, cries went up: "Save St. Valerie! Save St. Valerie!" Rescued by valiant local volunteer firefighters, St. Valerie was transported back to the rebuilt cathedral aboard a fire truck in a solemn procession, and every year during the long-established Firemen's Fair a special mass celebrates their heroism.

In the middle of Thibodaux right on Bayou Lafourche is the Wetlands Acadian Cultural Center of the Jean Lafitte National Park, with a theater and gallery for musical performances, art exhibits, periodic festivals, and living history demonstrations of early skills such as duck carving, net making, quilting, boat building, falconry, fly-tying, paddle carving, and shingle riving. This is a wonderful resource for visitors seeking to understand the Grand Dérangement and its lasting impact on the Louisiana bayou country. The French peasants who had farmed and fished in peace since the early 1600s along the Canadian coastal area later called Nova Scotia refused to swear loyalty to Britain when Acadia was ceded to that country under the Treaty of Utrecht in 1713. In 1755, England began the forcible expulsion of these Acadians, burned villages, seized properties, and crowded separated families into unseaworthy ships bound for British colonies in America. Many of the Acadians died on these desperate voyages, and those who survived were treated abominably everywhere they landed. Their efforts to reunite and rebuild lives, so movingly recorded in Longfellow's epic *Evangeline*, culminated with many coming together in Louisiana, its familiar French tongue and fertile farmland offering refuge and comfort to some three thousand exiles. Museum exhibits vividly tell

required to keep Lafourche's giant sugar plantations running smoothly. The surrounding fields are still planted with cane, but the workers' quarters stand silent and empty now, machinery having replaced the mule and plow, the field hand and hoe. Laurel Valley dates from the 1770s, and today there is a fascinating little museum in the old plantation store, its worn wood planks recalling the days when laborers were paid as little as $13 a month, often in script redeemable only at the company store. Today, the store is operated by the nonprofit Friends of Laurel Valley, formed to protect the site and direct rehabilitation of the surrounding structures, which have been used in filming a number of movies, including the story of Ray Charles in *Ray*.

Paddle carving

the story of their success in adapting their way of life to a new homeland with its differences in climate and culture, their resilience in wresting a subsistence living from the swamps and bayou wetlands, their tenacity in preserving their unique culture in the face of misguided assimilation efforts, and finally the emergence of Cajun chic, as a result of which their cooking and music and *joie de vivre* now enjoy national popularity and respect.

Across Bayou Lafourche is historic Laurel Valley Plantation, with one of the most complete collections of original dependencies and outbuildings in the state. The rows of cypress cabins are weathered and worn, their rusted tin roofs slanting uniformly in long rows and their gallery rails cobbled together of bits of mismatched wood, their steps caving in and doors to the adjoining outhouses ajar, yet they bear mute testimony to the enormity of the labor force and support facilities

Falconry

Orderly rows of slave quarters at Laurel Valley Plantation

E. D. WHITE HOUSE

Another governor of Louisiana lived just north of Thibodaux along LA 1, his simple raised cottage of hand-hewn pegged cypress, built in 1824, now a National Historic Landmark and state museum site. The Edward Douglass White House was home to a remarkable father-son pair. The first was a judge, state governor in the 1830s and three-term U.S. senator, the second not only a senator and member of the state supreme court, but also the only Louisianian to serve as chief justice of the U.S. Supreme Court. Today the E. D. White House contains exhibits examining the lives of these fascinating men, as well as the sugarcane industry and early Bayou Lafourche culture. Periodic special educational events and living history demonstrations are scheduled throughout the year.

In the glory days of the sugar empire, Bayou Lafourche was like a church aisle, the old saying went, with pews on both sides. And indeed there were Pughs on both sides of the bayou, the original three brothers who emigrated from the Carolinas around 1819—Dr. Whitmell; Augustin, the oldest; and Thomas, the youngest—married more Pughs, begat more Pughs, and expanded their landholdings to include more than two dozen big plantations. Before the Civil War, the Pughs owned at least 10 percent of the slaves in the Assumption-Lafourche Parish area, and their sugar production accounted for more than a tenth of the total production in the two-parish region.

The Pughs were leaders in the community and in the church. Dr. Whitmell Pugh's son, W.W. Pugh, served in the state legislature for several terms and was speaker of the house, parish superintendent of education, and a longtime police juror and levee board member. A colonel in the Assumption regiment of the Louisiana militia, he also helped found Christ Episcopal Church in Napoleonville, cutting the cypress and making the bricks on his Woodlawn Plantation for the lovely little church building. He

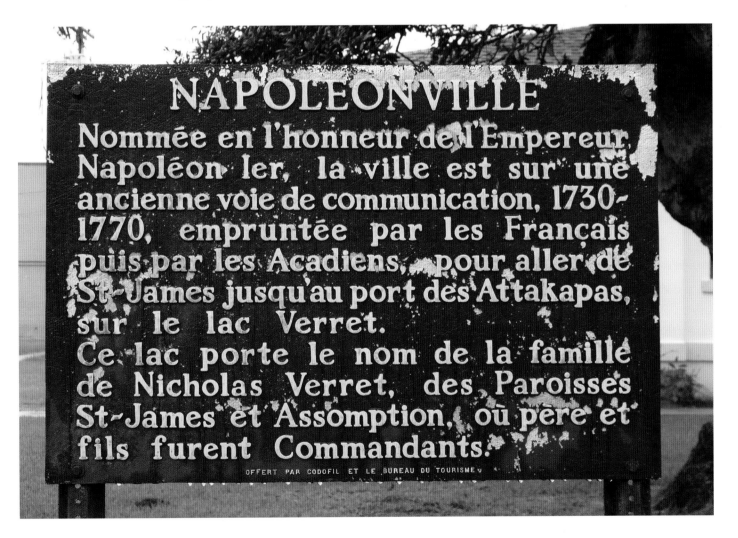

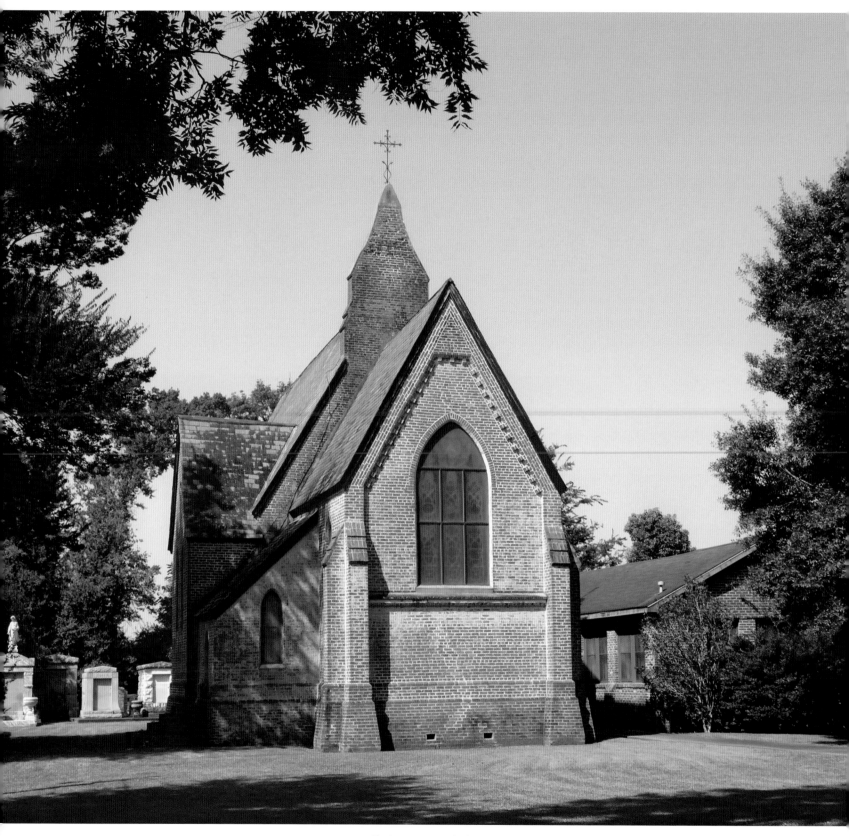

Christ Episcopal Church

Madewood Plantation

lived to the ripe old age of ninety-five, but in 1856 he lost a baby daughter and her nurse in the Isle Dernière hurricane, and his recorded reminiscences have come down in history as one of the most moving accounts of that terrible time.

Woodlawn is no more, but one magnificent Pugh home remains in testament to the days when sugar was king in this area, and the Pughs were its royal family. Considered one of the finest examples of pure Greek Revival in the South, Madewood, just across the bayou from LA 1, was begun in the mid-1840s, and designed by famed New Orleans architect Henry Howard. Its beautifully proportioned peaked pediment and heavily carved Ionic pillars give it the appearance of a great institution like a world bank or classic courthouse, but it was also designed to be a comfortable dwelling, sited on one of the highest spots along Bayou Lafourche to catch the cooling breezes off the waters with floor-to-ceiling windows, ceilings fifteen to twenty-four feet in height, and broad shaded galleries. Magnificent plaster moldings, twenty rooms, faux bois sliding pocket doors with etched glass panels, even a forty-eight-foot-long ballroom in one of two flanking wings provided an appropriate setting for Col. Thomas Pugh's family, which included fifteen children.

During the Civil War, Madewood was saved from destruction when Col. Pugh's plucky widow Eliza appealed to the Union general's Masonic ties with her late husband. The grounds were used as a hospital, but the house was spared. Not so lucky was Christ Episcopal Church, where Federal troops stabled their horses and used the Tiffany stained glass windows for target practice. One early Louisiana journalist, writing toward the end of the nineteenth century, described the church as one of the most

Trees arch over still bayou waters to create a tunnel effect.

Rustic cypress-shaded camps on Lake Verret

charming buildings in the South, and decried the fact that its abuse during the war left "the marrings of hoof and tooth still on the deep window ledges."

After decades of neglect, with hay stored in the beautiful ballroom, the Marshall family reclaimed Madewood, and still occupy it today, welcoming guests to take tours, to stay at the B&B, and to attend holiday feasts and musical soirees.

To the east are some of the River Road's most magnificent restored plantation homes, all open for tours, Greek Revival Oak Alley with its incredible live oaks, colorfully Creole Laura, St. Joseph with its long family heritage, and Whitney is being restored with an interpretive emphasis on slavery. A short side trip to the west from Napoleonville, the Attakapas Adventures swamp tour traverses Lake Verret—part

of the Elm Hall Wildlife Management Area of 2,800 acres owned by the Louisiana Department of Wildlife and Fisheries—at the extreme eastern edge of the Atchafalaya Basin. Here visitors see Louisiana's state wildflower, the iris; Louisiana's state bird, the brown pelican; and Louisiana's laid-back lifestyle, for the lake is lined with picturesque little camps and boat sheds shaded by immense cypress trees. The two or three-hour trips (sunset cruises and fishing charters are also available) on a comfortable twenty-foot pontoon boat with a licensed captain pass bald cypress and tupelo gums, a nineteenth-century logger's skidding camp, and lots of wildlife—anhingas and cormorants, bald eagles and osprey, herons, egrets, and all the creatures that make Louisiana's unspoiled swamp areas so popular with visitors from out of

Herons and egrets stalk through iris-studded waterways.

state. Of course, the alligators are the tourists' favorites, and Louisiana has a huge population of them since hunting is carefully controlled. In the early days, hunters harvesting gators at night, with spotlights, described alligator eyes shining from the waters in profusion as great the stars shining in the skies. Today, the Louisiana Department of Wildlife and Fisheries issues more than thirty thousand tags annually for hunters to legally take gators in the wild.

Donaldsonville

Donaldsonville's location, where Bayou Lafourche branches off from the Mississippi River, has proven to be both a blessing and a curse. It was an early, bustling hub of commercial activity along the river and bayou, and the town continues to be an industrial center. But it also attracted the ire of Yankees intent on inflicting punishment for Confederate harassment of Union naval activities on the Mississippi in the Donaldsonville area, which the Federals called "the piratical resort of all the bad men of the country."

Founded in 1806 by William Donaldson on the site of an early Chitimacha Indian village at the head of the bayou La Salle called La Fourche des Chetimaches, the town, the third to be incorporated in Louisiana, was the state capital for a single year, from January 1830 to January 1831, until the legislators found it too boring and moved back to New Orleans. Besides serving as an important trading post from the late-1700s and as the jump-off point for all traffic and trade going down Bayou Lafourche, as late at 1811 Donaldsonville was the only post office in the 190–mile stretch between New Orleans and Pinckneyville in the Mississippi Territory.

By the 1840s, Donaldsonville boasted a hand-powered ferry that "by laborious effort for nearly an hour" was capable of crossing the Mississippi with a skiff affixed to each side of a barge. The charges were twenty-five cents for foot passengers and $2 for gig and horse. By 1876, a steam ferry called the *Little Minnie* made the trip with an 8 hp motor and an upstream speed of eight mph. Horses and buggies or carriages could ride on the steamboat, and there was an attached flatboat for larger carts or wagons, mules, and stock.

The railroad had also reached Donaldsonville by 1876, though the local streets were in such bad condition after heavy rains that the newspaper editor wrote that he would rather stick a nail in his foot than walk to the train station after a rain. Improvements were quickly effected, and by 1871 the newspaper called the road to the depot a beautiful thoroughfare, though the editor immediately politicked for a more suitable street name than the original Indian moniker, "'Cabahanosse,' that polysyllabic monstrosity of ancient origin, fearful orthography and doubtful pronunciation." And so Cabahanosse (Choctaw Indian for "sleeping place of ducks") Street became the far less colorful Railroad Avenue. However, a local B&B/antiques purveyor carries on the original name today in a wonderful double-galleried 1890s structure, and brick sidewalks added to the ease of perambulating about town.

Bikur Sholim Cemetery contains graves of early Jewish immigrants.

Italianate B. Lemann & Bro. Building

After the Civil War, the town's recovery was facilitated by a large population of Jewish immigrants, whose business skills were vital in the days after Reconstruction. Bikur Sholim Cemetery, founded in 1856, contains more than 120 graves, some with inscriptions in Hebrew. Many of the Jewish immigrants were from Alsace-Lorraine on the Franco-German border. Seeking to escape oppression in the Old World, they arrived in successive waves beginning in the early 1800s. Many followed the cotton empire from the depleted lands of the East Coast to the South. Often beginning as peddlers with their wares in packs on their backs or in small pushcarts, they

settled along major river trade routes and thrived not only economically but also socially and politically. Donaldsonville had more than seventy families worshipping in its synagogue, and the town had more Jewish mayors than any other in the South.

The B. Lemann & Bro. Building, built on Railroad Avenue in 1877 by Bernard and Myer Lemann to house the mercantile business started by their father Jacob Lemann in 1836, stands as a testament to the significance of the Jewish contribution to the society and economy of Donaldsonville. Designed by noted New Orleans architect James Freret in the ornate Italianate style, the 60,000-square-foot stuc-

River Road African-American Museum

coed brick building has a colonnade of fluted cast-iron columns supporting an overhanging gallery on three sides. At one time, it was the oldest continuously operated family-owned department store in the state, proffering groceries both retail and wholesale, men's and ladies' clothing, piece goods, notions and hardware. When Jacob Lehmann died in 1887, his obituary called him one of the largest planters and property holders in Ascension Parish, who owed

his "advancement to combined shrewdness, industry and integrity, for no man could prosper as he did and retain the friendship and respect of all with whom he had dealings, had not his business methods been conducted upon a plane of strict justice and honor. He and his sons have made the name of Lemann a symbol of all that is honorable in the business world."

The Historic Donaldsonville Museum and welcome center presently has extensive exhibits on local history in the picturesque Lemann Building, including Jacob Lemann's well-used rolltop desk. Nearby, the River Road African-American Museum focuses on the contributions of antebellum slaves and free persons of color, including Pierre Caliste Landry, the nation's first black mayor. A large National Register-listed Historic District of 635 structures includes buildings both great and small, most dating from after the Civil War; Lessard Street, parallel to Railroad Avenue, boasts rows of big impressive homes at the river end and rows of small shotgun houses gussied up with Victorian trim at the other end.

The reason most of Donaldsonville's historic homes post-date the Civil War is that the town was essentially leveled in 1862. When Confederate cavalrymen operating near Donaldsonville fired upon and harassed Union ships on the Mississippi, Adm. David Farragut threatened to bombard Donaldsonville if the sniping continued. When it persisted, Farragut ordered the town evacuated and opened fire from several gunboats on August 9, then landed a party of Federal troops to burn what was left standing. Over two-thirds of the town was demolished and Donaldsonville was reduced to "a desert of smoke-blackened ruins, nearly all in ashes." The following month, even Union naval officer Lt. Francis A. Roe, commanding the U.S. gunboat *Katahdin*, harshly criticized the Federal troops who, sent into Donaldsonville to obtain sugar for commissaries, instead pillaged a large mansion near the landing, carrying off silver, liquor and even ladies' clothing. This prompted Lt. Roe to write to General Butler, "I am desirous of encountering enemies and of injuring them in every manly manner . . . but it is disgraceful and humiliating to be ordered on guard duty of soldiers employed in pillaging ladies' dresses and petticoats."

In the fall of that same year, using the labor of liberated plantation slaves, Federal troops began construction at Donaldsonville of a star-shaped earthen fort surrounded by an impassable open moat sixteen feet wide and twelve feet deep. Called Fort Butler for Gen. Benjamin Butler, Union occupier of New Orleans, it was located on the west bank of Bayou Lafourche close to the river. Gen. Alfred Mouton, in command of the Confederate forces of the Lafourche district in the absence of Gen. Richard Taylor, could ill afford to have Yankees controlling the mouth of Bayou Lafourche.

Fort Butler was garrisoned with fewer than two hundred troops, many of them convalescents wounded at Port Hudson. Maj. Joseph D. Bullen of the 18th Maine also commanded companies of the 28th Maine and the 16th New Hampshire as well as men from the 1st Louisiana Regiment of Native Guards (Union) and several other regiments with the assistance of Maj. Henry M. Port of the 7th Vermont. In June 1863, the outnumbered Union forces stationed there, with heavy firepower support from gunboats on the river, repulsed a Confederate cavalry assault led by Brig. Gen. Thomas Green. Casualties among the cavalrymen trying to cross the open moat and scale fort walls were heavy, and fighting was so desperate that at one point combatants even threw bricks at each other. Said one observer after the battle was over, "The sun rose upon a ghastly sight, upon green slopes gray with the dead, the dying and the maimed, and the black ditch red with their blood."

This was one of the first battles to utilize black troops, who in previous engagements had frequently found themselves relegated to building bridges, digging ditches, even harvesting sugar crops as if they were hired hands rather than soldiers, even on the Union side. Prejudice wore not just gray in the Civil War era, but also blue, and many Union officers refused to command black troops.

Union gunboats shelled Donaldsonville repeatedly in June 1863 in the aftermath of the Battle of Fort Butler. With its homes pillaged and burned, its crops confiscated or ruined, and property damage estimated at around $300 million, few cities paid such a high price as Donaldsonville.

At one end of Lessard St. are small shotguns with fanciful Victorian trim.

At the other end of Lessard St. are larger, more impressive Victorians.

On the monument (left panel):

"WE ARE STILL ANXIOUS, AS WE HAVE EVER BEEN, TO SHOW THE WORLD THAT THE LATENT COURAGE OF THE AFRICAN IS AROUSED, AND THAT, WHILE FIGHTING UNDER THE AMERICAN FLAG, WE CAN AND WILL BE A WALL OF FIRE AND DEATH TO THE ENEMIES OF THIS COUNTRY, OUR BIRTHPLACE."

CAPTAIN JAMES H. INGRAHAM
1st REGIMENT OF THE
LOUISIANA NATIVE GUARDS

On the monument (right panel):

"THIS FORTIFICATION IS A SYMBOL OF THE AFRICAN AMERICAN CONTRIBUTION TO THEIR OWN FREEDOM. NOT ONLY DID BLACK HANDS CONSTRUCT THIS CITADEL, BUT AFRICAN AMERICAN SOLDIERS HELPED IN ITS DEFENSE."

DONALD S. FRAZIER
ASSISTANT PROFESSOR
McMURRY UNIVERSITY
ABILENE, TEXAS

Monument marking the location of Fort Butler and commemorating black troops

To the south, the plantations of Belle Alliance and St. Emma, both owned at the time by Charles Kock, would be the scene of the last battles in the Lafourche district, though there would be small skirmishes in the area throughout the remainder of the war. The fall of the last Confederate strongholds on the Mississippi River at Vicksburg and Port Hudson gave Union forces complete control of river traffic and made any Confederate presence in the nearby bayou country impossible to sustain. Monuments mark the location of Fort Butler and commemorate the valiant participation of black troops in the battle.

This is also the end of Bayou Lafourche, or the beginning, and from this point northward, LA 1 follows the Mighty Mississippi rather than the bayou. Thousands of years ago, the Mississippi took the Lafourche channel as its main route to the gulf, and every spring, as snow melted upriver, it overflowed its banks and spread rich nutrients and sediment across the floodplain. Higher land built up along the channel due to these deposits, land that was so rich and productive it naturally attracted both small farmers and big planters as the Lafourche area was gradually settled beginning in the late 1700s. But even as the crops thrived, floods periodically wiped them out. Levees were insubstantial affairs erected by individual planters, often incapable of containing the torrent of spring floodwaters, and crevasses or levee breaks meant planters lost an entire year's production, structures, livestock, and sometimes even their lives.

So it was decided in 1902-3, upon the advice of engineers, that Bayou Lafourche should be disconnected from the Mississippi's present channel, and the dam subsequently erected at Donaldsonville certainly helped to decrease the local danger of flooding. But the bayou was left stagnant and dying, so it was eventually reconnected to the Mississippi by artificial means, a series of pipes and pumps visible from the Fort Butler site that allow controlled flow of river water down the bayou. Now there are plans for increasing that flow, for the bayoulands benefitted more than they knew from the river's overflow, and only recently has it been recognized how much the swamps and marshes have withered without the annual enrichment.

Headwaters of Bayou Lafourche at Donaldsonville, where pumps control flow from the Mississippi.

Capital

White Castle

Along this stretch, LA 1 most closely parallels the Mississippi River. One immense plantation, running from roadway to levee, is all that is left of a sugarcane empire that at its peak of production contained more than seven thousand acres. This is the magnificent Nottoway, its white castle the largest extant plantation home in the South, planned and built over a decade from 1849 to 1859 in the last gasp of antebellum glory.

Nottoway was built to house the large family of aristocratic planter John Hampden Randolph, descended from a long and distinguished line of Virginia barristers and burgesses. He had eleven children, seven of them daughters, and only such a spectacular structure could provide a suitable setting for them. The statistics are staggering: fifty-three thousand square feet under the slate roof, sixty-four rooms, two hundred windows, a doorway for each day of the year, sixteen fireplaces, seven interior stairways, twenty-six built-in closets and innovative indoor bathrooms with hot and cold running water fed by a ten thousand-gallon cistern atop the roof, all seamlessly combined by noted architect Henry Howard in a marvelous manor with a unique combination of Greek Revival and Italianate influences unlike any other along the Great River Road.

A rear *garçonnière* housed the boys above the age of fourteen to keep them from offending their sisters' sensibilities. A side wing held the seven Randolph girls, each of whom (except one who died young) married in the home's famous sixty-five-foot White Ballroom, with its Corinthian columns supporting triple arches, elaborate plaster frieze work, curved exterior walls, and everything from floor to ceiling sparkling white to set off to best advantage the radiant brides' beauty.

During the Civil War, Randolph removed himself and his slaves to Texas to grow cotton to support the family, while his wife faced down Union soldiers from the front gallery with a dagger tucked in her belt. The home was spared when a Union officer, aboard a federal gunboat firing from the river, recognized it as one in which he had previously been entertained and ordered the bombardment to cease. Now on the National Register of Historic Places, Nottoway is a popular B&B and a setting for weddings and receptions. It has a fine restaurant and offers tours daily.

Statue in Nottoway's gardens

Wildflowers on the Mississippi River levee brighten the view of immense antebellum Nottoway Plantation.

Plaquemine

Location, location, location. The little communities that developed at the confluence of bayou and river waters were defined by their sites, none more so than Plaquemine, established where Bayou Plaquemine meets the Mississippi. They call this bayou the passageway of the Acadians, who were deported from their homes in Nova Scotia beginning in 1755 and struggled to reunite and rebuild their lives in Louisiana's southwestern prairies. Mentioned as early as 1699 in Iberville's journals and named for the numerous persimmon trees along its banks—whose beauties were extolled in Longfellow's epic poem *Evangeline*—Bayou Plaquemine was vital to inland settlement and the flow of regional commerce.

It became the northern terminus of the Intracoastal Canal system after a lock was erected to control bayou water levels, ease movement of boat traffic from one water level to another, and provide a shortcut from the river into the state's interior heartland. Prior to the lock's opening, the mouth of the bayou was often impassable and clogged with logjams. Shortly after the Civil War, Bayou Plaquemine was completely shut off from the river to halt interior flooding, but the demands of the booming timber and fishing industries necessitated opening a convenient channel between the harvest areas of the Atchafalaya Basin and the processing areas along the Mississippi.

Construction of the Plaquemine Lock was called a three-year job that took fourteen years and bankrupted seven contractors due to a huge assortment of problems, including soil instability and yellow

Plaquemine Lock

The gleaming white Plaquemine Lockhouse shows Dutch architectural influence.

Bayou Plaquemine Waterfront Park

fever epidemics. Completed in 1909 as the highest freshwater lift lock in the world (fifty-one feet) with a unique gravity-flow design, the lock was later modernized with hydraulic pumps, and steam power greatly reduced the amount of time required to equalize water levels. The first steamboat to enter the lock was the *Carrie B. Schwing*, used by the Schwing Lumber and Shingle Company to transport lumberjacks. On April 9, 1909, Miss Carrie herself christened the lock by breaking a bottle of champagne against its wall. By traversing the route through the lock to the Atchafalaya waterways system, shippers cut more than one hundred miles from the route to the Gulf, and during World War II, when there were fears of enemy submarines penetrating the Mississippi, lock traffic greatly increased as shipping was diverted to inland waterways.

Today the Plaquemine Lock, restored as a state historic site and listed on the National Register of Historic Places, serves as the focal point of a bustling downtown area and often hosts interpretive events. The little lockhouse of gleaming white tile so bright it was used as a navigation aid for river traffic has unique Dutch-style architecture with stepped parapet gables and round windows that used to house steam boilers. The Dutch influence stemmed from lock designer Col. George W. Goethals, later chief engineer for the Panama Canal. Today the building serves as a museum and visitor center. An open-air pavilion houses historic boats—house boats, wooden *bateaux*, dugout *pirogues*, Lafitte skiffs, even a peculiar take-apart boat that could be dismantled and carried on a small plane—representative of the thousands of river craft that passed through the lock during its fifty-two years of operation. The lock overlooks the beautiful award-winning Bayou Plaquemine Waterfront Park, offering pier walkways along the bayou, covered pavilion and scenic overlooks, boating, fishing, and birdwatching.

Across the street from the lock is the Iberville Museum, housed in a columned Greek Revival structure built in 1848 as a parish courthouse and later used as city hall. Artifacts on exhibit include the original incorporation papers of the city of Plaquemine dated 1835, an old horse-drawn buggy called a Jumper because it bounced across canefields on its four-foot-tall wheels like it was jumping over the rows, a Model T, and a twenty-four-foot cypress *bateau* with a Nadler putt-putt two-cycle engine made in Plaquemine. These are supplemented by a video produced by renowned local historian Tony Fama and moving military displays, including World War II telegram death notices to servicemen's families and a Japanese container used to ship home a POW's possessions.

Nearby, the imposing St. John the Evangelist Catholic Church is called the south's purest example of Italian Romanesque architecture, with an impressive balastrino altar of marble and handsome campanile. The old railroad depot houses a market bringing together area artists and other vendors. It is among more than one hundred structures of varying architectural styles included in Plaquemine's downtown National Register Historic District. While a train still runs through town and sugarcane still dominates the landscape south of town, along the river the petrochemical industry, led by Dow Chemical— one of the state's largest—has taken the place of many of the smaller factories and foundries. Nearby Old Turnerville features some picturesque nineteenth-century structures along the river.

Residents of Plaquemine mark the passing

Iberville Museum

One of many large-scale petroleum processing plants found along LA 1 and the Mississippi River.

seasons by checking out the snazzy outfits on the Schwing gorilla, the beloved local icon which reigns over LA 1 as it cruises through town. While the mistress of the house was not overly thrilled when a forklift, at her husband's instigation, first unloaded the immense creature in her front yard, she rose to the challenge and had her dressmaker concoct gorilla fashions, from elaborate Mardi Gras regalia to pilgrim and Easter bunny costumes, even snorkels and flippers and swim trunks for summer. Ah yes, humor has saved many a marriage! And in Cajun Country, *cher*, even gorillas know how to pass a good time, and in style, yeah.

The iconic Schwing gorilla

Port Allen

The best views of the imposing monolith of the state capitol building at Baton Rouge are from the western side of the river, and the riverside park also provides a great spot for watching the traffic along the Mississippi River, which drains some thirty-one states and two Canadian provinces in its 2,340-mile journey from its source in Minnesota. The largest river in the country in terms of volume of water flow, the Mississippi was the nation's primary trade route until the Civil War, and even today there is a steady stream of sturdy tugboats pushing strings of as many as forty barges up or down the river. Each barge typically holds up to 1,500 tons of cargo, fifteen times more than a railroad car can hold and sixty times more than a tractor-trailer truckload. Nearly four hundred million tons of cargo move along the Mississippi River each year.

Along this section of LA 1, the industrial and chemical plants stretching south along the Mississippi's west bank attest to the importance of the river for transportation even today in Louisiana, which is home to some two hundred refineries and petrochemical plants. The Port Allen Lock on the heavily trafficked Gulf Intracoastal Waterway, completed in 1961 when the Plaquemine Lock proved inadequate to handle large vessels, has annual average lockages in excess of six thousand, passing more than twenty-five million tons into this remarkable east-west inland transportation artery linking deepwater ports, tributaries, rivers, and bayous along the entire Gulf of Mexico coast.

By traversing the Port Allen to Morgan City route of the Intracoastal rather than the Mississippi River, tugs, barges, and other vessels cut 160 miles off the journey to the coast. Hence, the Port of Greater Baton Rouge, channeling its traffic through the Port Allen Lock, ranks among the top ten ports in the country. The nation's farthest-inland deepwater port, the Port of Greater Baton Rouge has extensive agricultural facilities at its site along the river in

The Louisiana State Capitol as seen from Port Allen on the west bank over a string of coal barges travelling along the Mississippi River.

Port Allen, including a grain elevator, several sugar warehouses capable of holding eighty thousand tons of raw sugar, a flour mill grinding 360 tons of wheat daily, an 8.5-acre coffee roasting and packaging facility, a molasses terminal which is the state's premier fructose transfer facility for the soft-drink industry, and an animal-feed production and distribution operation.

There were a number of large plantations along this stretch of LA 1, and one that is still accessible to the public by reservation for special events is exuberantly ornate Poplar Grove. Its main house is a colorful Oriental pavilion that was built for the 1884 World's Industrial and Cotton Centennial Exposition in New Orleans and transported upriver by barge to its present location along the levee north of Port Allen. While the last working sugar mill in West Baton Rouge Parish, the big 1855 Cinclaire Plantation mill, ground its last load of cane in 2005, plenty of sugarcane is still planted on these flat fertile fields.

The West Baton Rouge Museum is the best place to gain a comprehensive understanding of the entire sugar producing process. In the museum's main gallery, a twenty-two-foot handcrafted working model of a sugar mill reproduces the process in fascinating detail. This incredible model was built in 1904 for the Louisiana Purchase Exposition in St. Louis. A video covers the history of the sugar industry from its beginnings in downtown New Orleans, when Etienne de Boré in 1795 first produced granulated sugar on what is now Audubon Park, through the development of the vacuum evaporation process by a French-educated Creole a decade later to the boom years that came with the introduction of new technology, better refining processes, disease-resistant cane, and more environmentally conscious farming practices.

On museum grounds are a 1937 shotgun house constructed from scraps of an old boxcar, the beauti-

The Aillet House on the grounds of the West Baton Rouge Museum

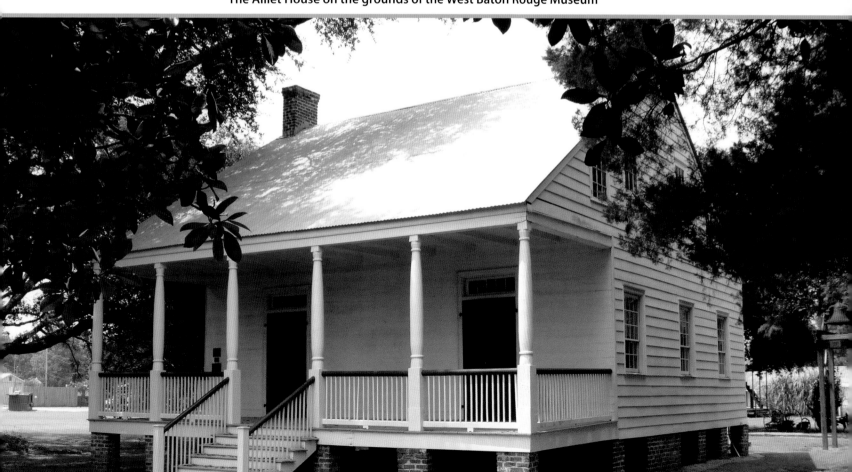

West Baton Rouge Museum

fully restored 1830 French Creole Aillet House, an Acadian sharecropper's cabin, and an antebellum double-pen slave cabin from Allendale Plantation, once owned by Louisiana's Civil War governor Gen. Henry Watkins Allen for whom the town is named. These structures tell in vivid detail the story of the early sugar planters in the plantation big houses with their formal parlors and four-poster beds, and, in contrast, the fieldhands in their rustic cypress dwellings, cooking on open hearths, sleeping on moss or cornshuck-stuffed pallets on the floor beneath mosquito nets, amusing the children with simple shuck dolls and marbles made of clay. The museum has a mule-powered sugar mill to periodically demonstrate the earliest grinding methods and hosts an annual fall Sugarfest celebrating the sugar harvest, with nineteenth-century crafts, hands-on history, and plenty of food, music, and fun.

Louisiana's Civil War governor Henry Watkins Allen's statue surveys the governmental complex at the heart of Port Allen.

New Roads

While Acadiana has its eternal tragedy embodied in the story of star-crossed lovers separated on their wedding day in the cruel dispersal of Acadians from Nova Scotia, doomed to seek each other through a lifetime of wandering lives, and reunited only in death as immortalized in Longfellow's lengthy epic poem *Evangeline*, New Roads has its own tragic love story with contemporary implications in the life and death of Julien Poydras.

Statesman, philanthropist, educator, planter, and merchant, Poydras was born in 1740 in Nantes, France, and he lost his heart to a young maiden of a family too poor to provide the requisite dowry and thus was unable to marry. Heartbroken, he joined the French navy, was captured by the British, escaped, and eventually made his way to America, where he began working as a peddler before eventually becoming the owner of a number of plantations with extensive trading connections. In the late 1700s, he built the house on Alma Plantation, where Pointe Coupée's last working sugar mill survives today. He was a director of the first bank in Louisiana, New Orleans' Banque de la Louisiane that opened in 1805 in his Vieux Carré home (which would later house the world-famous Brennan's Restaurant), endowed some of the state's earliest institutions of learning, and represented the area in the United States Congress. He has been called the father of public education in Louisiana, and his epitaph proclaims, "Lover of his adopted country, faithful citizen and public officer, munificent donor to charitable funds."

In spite of his outstanding accomplishments, Julien Poydras never married, nor did he ever forget his first love. When he died in 1824 at the age of eighty, he left in his will an endowment to provide dowries for all the area brides, "the unfortunate always to be preferred." Over the years many local lasses from West Baton Rouge and Pointe Coupée parishes benefitted from his generosity. Poydras rests in peace in front of the 22,000-square-foot Julien Poydras School, built in 1924 as a public elementary and high school, now preserved as a center for cultural and artistic endeavors and performances. On the grounds is the diminutive cypress post office formerly used in nearby Mix, Louisiana, considered the smallest postal facility in the country.

Poydras' monument overlooks False River, *Fausse Rivière*, a picturesque oxbow lake formed by a twenty-two-mile loop cut off when the Mississippi River took a straighter short cut, giving the parish its name, Pointe Coupée. In the late 1600s, early French explorers from LaSalle to Iberville and Bienville visited the area and Indian guides showed them

Tiny Mix post office

False River

the overland shortcut that the river eventually followed. Around 1729, the French established a fort
in the area, making this one of the state's earliest settlements, and, by 1738, the first church, St. Francis
of Pointe Coupée, had been erected. When Spanish
authorities constructed a road connecting the Mississippi and False River around 1776, the settlement
took its name from this *Chemin Neuf* or new road.

Today weekend camps and some very upscale
homes line False River and the Fourth of July boat
parade celebrates the joys of life lived on the water in
easygoing Louisiana style. Mardi Gras day features
other beloved and long-established parades, only on
dry land down the main street. Here in the town
of New Roads, with its quaint little shops and nice
restaurants overlooking the lake, may be found the
small U.S. Coast and Geodetic Survey marker on
the grounds of the Scott Civic Center proclaim-
ing this exact spot, 30.699270 degrees latitude and
−91.457133 degrees longitude, the state center of
population as of 2000 when the head count was
4,468,976. The hurricanes of 2005 no doubt shifted
sufficient folks around to move the next center else-
where.

Also here in the fertile fields of Pointe Coupée,

**U.S. Census marker designated Port Allen the state's center
of population in 2000.**

Riverlake Plantation

cotton meets sugarcane as the crops start to shift dominance, and the sugarcane so prolific in south Louisiana begins to give way to the cotton crop that is predominant in the central parishes. When early Louisiana journalist Martha R. Field described Pointe Coupée for the New Orleans *Daily Picayune* in the late nineteenth century, she wrote with characteristic colorfulness:

> Almost midway in the center of the state, cut into fantastic shape by the twists of the river, this is a parish that is like a shield, with one side gold and the other silver. It is here that the cotton and the sugarcane meet, and often the wind lifts the long snowy banners from the one field and loops them, frayed and feather-light, on the purple scepters of the other. It is here the smokes of the cotton gin and sugar mill marry in the sky.

Early plantations in this area include the raised Creole cottage called Riverlake, birthplace of Louisiana author Ernest Gaines. The unadorned realities of plantation workers' lives in the rustic quarters provide the backdrop for many of his most moving works, including *A Gathering of Old Men* and *The Autobiography of Miss Jane Pittman*.

PARLANGE

Parlange, the most impressive of Pointe Coupée plantations, is open to the public for tours by advance reservation. The French marquis Claude Vincent de Ternant built it in 1750 and direct descendants still occupy it. A rambling French Creole structure encircled by broad double galleries and built of cypress insulated with *bousillage*, it is a National Historic Landmark and one of Louisiana's oldest architectural treasures, filled with magnificent original furnishings and exceptionally fine family portraits. Indigo, sugarcane, cotton, corn, soybeans, and cattle have been raised on its extensive fields, and it remains a working farm. The marquis' daughter-in-law saved the house during occupations by both Union and Confederate forces during the Civil War, and it was her daughter, Marie Virginie de Ternant Avegno, who was the beautiful subject of painter John Singer Sargent's bold masterpiece called *Portrait of Madame X*, which scandalized Parisian society of the 1880s. Today's plantation mistress, "Miss Lucy" Parlange, Louisiana's legendary grande dame, still exudes warmth and graciousness, though she might not be able to clamber to the top of the hayloft with visiting children quite as gleefully as she once did. Then again, knowing the irrepressible Miss Lucy, she just might.

Pointe Coupée Parish Museum and Tourist Center is in a restored tenant cabin from Parlange.

Across LA 1 from the main Parlange house, one of its tenant cabins, built around 1800, has been beautifully restored and enlarged as the Pointe Coupée Parish Museum and Tourist Center. Constructed of handsawn timbers dovetailed at the corners and secured by wooden pegs, the structure, which has simple, authentic early furnishings including a wonderful large loom, dispenses tourist information daily.

Morganza

Above New Roads, the rural area is sparsely populated. The rich river plantations that harvested immense acreages of indigo and sugarcane give way to less imposing structures, simple rude cabins abandoned amidst the desolation of wide-open fields, tin-roofed cypress barns rotting from disuse, vines clambering over antebellum cotton gins long since forsaken. And yet, in the decades since the release of the 1969 counterculture road trip movie *Easy Rider*, some of its most shocking scenes filmed along the levee road and in a small café right on LA 1 in Morganza, the ravages of time have been etched more harshly on the faces of the movie's young stars—Peter Fonda, Dennis Hopper, and Jack Nicholson—than on the timeless landscapes of flat treeless cane and cotton fields interspersed with small weather-beaten country stores and the sleepy small railroad communities that surround them.

The little town of Morganza, named after early 1800s settler Charles Morgan, has a fine antique shop specializing in Victorian pieces, a wonderful café called Not Your Mama's descended from New Roads' famous upscale restaurant called Ma Mama's, and an impeccably maintained Catholic church, but visitors are disappointed to find only cement steps leading to a vacant lot marking the location where Hollywood came to call. The little row of commercial structures next to the lot provide a feel for what is missing, however, typical small railroad-community storefront businesses just like *Easy Rider*'s famous café, Melancon's, run by the late Mrs. Blackie Hebert who is shown standing behind the counter

in the film. Mrs. Hebert's daughter Elida was one of the teenaged girls in the infamous café scene, and the good ol' boys included such illustrious citizens as the town mayor, sheriff, high school principal, horticulturist, a construction worker, and Elida's then-fiancé who would die of complications from Agent Orange exposure in Vietnam. The local folks were not given a script, just told to talk, and they were all dismayed when the final cuts made them look like such country bumpkins. Elida recalls that the girls made about $25 for their efforts, and her mother was paid just a couple of thousand dollars to close the café to walk-in business for the day of filming. Elida's line of dialogue, as the girls giggled together and speculated about the three strangers, was "The white shirt's for me," alluding to Peter Fonda, and after the filming Fonda would indeed take her on a long motorcycle ride. But the local populace was not overly impressed with the Hollywood stars or with the Hell's Angels who accompanied them to maintain the motorcycles used in the movie.

Along this stretch of LA 1, travelers get a feel for the massive efforts required to alleviate flooding and control the flow of the Mississippi River. Main-tained by the U.S. Army Corps of Engineers since the 1950s, the Morganza Spillway was designed to absorb some of the river's overflow floodwaters to protect downstream communities. Further upriver, the complex of locks and dams called the Old River Control Structures struggle to keep the Mississippi from changing course and jumping into the Atchafalaya River. In this area, the Father of Waters has already cut off some sharp curves to strand whole islands of property, most notably Raccourci Island and Turnbull Island, from West Feliciana Parish across the river and has left them physically attached to Pointe Coupée Parish.

The Mississippi River, which over the past few thousand years has meandered among several routes to the Gulf in its quest for the shortest straightest course, has been tempted by the Atchafalaya channel for years. In 1831, Capt. Henry Shreve made a misguided attempt to shorten the distance to the Gulf of Mexico by straightening out a big loop in the Mississippi called Turnbull's Bend. Turnbull's Bend was where the Red River flowed into the Mississippi, just above where the Atchafalaya River flowed out of it. Shreve's Cut meant the Red River would

flow into the Atchafalaya instead, and by 1951 it became clear that the Mississippi wanted to take the same westward course, with potentially catastrophic environmental and economic results. Congress authorized the U.S. Army Corps of Engineers to keep that from happening by constructing the Old River Control Project, named for the river channel abandoned by the Mississippi due to Shreve's Cut. The Control Structures maintain the balance of flow between the rivers and allow boat passage between the Mississippi, Atchafalaya, and Red rivers through the lock and dam.

Though harnessed by the Corps within ever-higher levees, preventing catastrophic flooding in populated areas but also preventing the beneficial cyclical spreading of overflow sediment that used to renew surrounding lands, the powerful Mississippi River will always have a mind of its own. Said old river pilot turned author Mark Twain, "Ten thousand River Commissions with the mines of the world at their back cannot tame that lawless stream, cannot curb it or confine it, cannot say to it, Go here, or Go there, and make it obey; cannot save a shore which it has sentenced; cannot bar its path with an obstruction which it will not tear down, dance over and laugh at."

Innis *and* Simmesport

"On fame's eternal camping ground
Their silent tents are spread
And glory guards with solemn sound
The bivouac of the dead."

So reads the inscription on the monument "sacred to the valor and patriotism of the Confederate warriors of Pointe Coupée," topped by a statue of a bearded soldier surveying a burial ground in which many of his comrades rest in peace. This is St. Stephen's Episcopal Church in Innis, a beautiful English-style Gothic Episcopal church with its peaceful cemetery of picturesque tombs surrounded by wrought iron fences and shaded by giant sweet olive trees. The church was founded in 1848 as the first

solid-brick building in Pointe Coupée; the bricks were slave-made, and Charles Duncan Stewart, who lies buried just behind the church, transferred the title of the property to the rector and wardens "for the sum of $1 cash."

Consecrated in 1859 by Bishop Leonidas Polk, the Fighting Bishop of the Confederacy, St. Stephen's had the first boy choir and the first woman layreader in the diocese, and its congregation included over the years many distinguished citizens, including one of the church founders, Dr. John George Archer who "ended his well-spent and useful life" in the 1880s saying "Simply to thy cross I cling," according to his tombstone. Also notable is Dr. William Bisland Archer, born in 1853, who died of yellow fever at

St. Stephen's Episcopal Church

St. Stephen's Confederate monument surveys surrounding graves of fallen comrades.

Greenville, Miss., where he had gone to assist the sufferers. Lovely little St. Stephen's has been restored and is listed on the National Register of Historic Places.

On the levee road, St. Stephen's monument to the unknown Confederate soldier is but one of a number of Civil War sites along this stretch of LA 1, for quite a few small battles were fought here in the spring of 1864. Fort De Russy was a Confederate stronghold defending the lower Red River valley when Gen. A. J. Smith's Union army attacked in March of 1864, and the Battle of Yellow Bayou was fought on May 18, above where LA 1 crosses the Atchafalaya River into Simmesport. Also called the Battle of Norwood's Plantation, this was the last battle of Union General Banks' Red River campaign, in which Confederate Gen. Richard Taylor's forces failed to keep the Union army from crossing the Atchafalaya River here. Today, Yellow Bayou Park, which provides picnic pavilions and other facilities along the banks of the picturesque bayou, is the setting for the Atchafalaya River Festival and other events.

Yellow Bayou Park

Mansura

The town was incorporated in 1860, but its main claim to fame lately has been more culinary than historic, and when Mansura celebrated its centennial in 1960, it had the Louisiana state legislature officially declare it "La Capitale de Cochon de Lait." Today the popular annual Cochon de Lait Festival draws enthusiastic crowds to the well-planned festival grounds to feast on roast suckling pig.

Next door is La Maison DesFossé, one of the oldest structures extant in Avoyelles Parish and the first to be recognized as significant enough for listing on the National Register of Historic Places. A simple French Colonial structure, it took its name from Mansura's second mayor, Dr. Jules Charles DesFossé. Dr. DesFossé was a dentist who came to Louisiana from France, and after he purchased this property in 1850, he and his wife Celestine Bordelon used it as their primary residence as well as his medical office. Typical of early homes of the region, the DesFossé House has walls of *bousillage* and bricks made of local clay. Today, it is open for tours three days a week.

La Maison DesFossé

Marksville

A broken wagon wheel in 1794 led Marcos Litche, a travelling peddler born in Venice, Italy, to stop awhile, and the friendliness of the resident Native Americans and other early settlers persuaded him never to leave. The trading post he established, first called Marc's Place, then Marc's Store, and finally Marc's Ville, gave the town its name. He settled down, married, obtained Spanish land grants of more than four hundred arpents, and donated most of the courthouse square centering Marksville's present pretty downtown area.

Many of the early settlers here in Avoyelles Parish were of French descent, as you can tell from the names of the little towns like Moreauville, but this is just about as far north as what one early Louisiana writer called the "fragrantly French" influence extends. The 1820s Hypolite Bordelon home, right on LA 1 at the northern end of town, has been restored in tribute to their contributions. This typical early Creole dwelling, built by one of the pioneering families of this area, with its cypress picket fence and outbuildings, has been restored and authentically furnished as headquarters for the local Chamber of Commerce and is on the National Register of Historic Places. Its double-pitch roof is an unusual feature, but the house plan is typical, with two large

Simple cypress Hypolite Bordelon home

Picturesque utilitarian outbuildings flank the Hypolite Bordelon house.

rooms around a central chimney, back and front porches, and one small *cabinet* room in the rear.

The validated history of the Marksville area goes back farther than its earliest European-born visitors, as is shown at the Marksville State Historic Site, a forty-two-acre ceremonial site strategically located on a bluff which is the highest point for thirty miles, overlooking that ancient channel of the Mississippi now called Old River. It is considered by archaeologists to be of unique national significance in interpreting and understanding the prehistoric Native American culture in this area. On this site more than two thousand years ago flourished what is known as the Marksville culture, a southeastern variant of the more famous Hopewell culture centered in Ohio. The Marksville culture, 100-400 AD, was characterized by elaborate mortuary ceremonialism, conical burial mounds, complex trade networks, and decorative pottery.

Recognized as a National Historic Landmark in 1964, the importance of the Marksville site was not established until investigations of the area began in the 1920s with a Smithsonian Institute study. Preserved on the state site today is an earthen embankment 3,300 feet long and up to seven feet tall in places, enclosing forty acres and a number of mounds, including a flat-topped one 300 feet in diameter and several conical ones up to twenty feet tall, believed to have had burial and ceremonial purposes. The Native Americans did not have metal tools, so these mounds were constructed by digging with sticks to fill baskets with earth, and then piling up thousands and thousands of basketfuls. The excavated burial mounds yielded stone projectile points, scrapers, hammer stones, decorated potsherds, clay vessels and pipes, stone knives, and other evidences of a sophisticated prehistoric culture.

The museum on this state historic site, with its open landscaped central courtyard, has explanatory exhibits and a number of excavated artifacts. The site provides picnic facilities and hiking trails, periodic special events, and interpretive programs on archae-

Marksville State Historic Site preserves prehistoric Native American burial and ceremonial mounds.

TUNICA - BILOXI
INDIAN RESERVATION
c. 1790
·:·
Lands granted to the
Tunica tribe by the Spanish
government comprise part of the
present reservation. The
Tunica-Biloxi Tribe is a fusion
of Tunica, Biloxi, Ofo, and
Avoyel peoples.

opened in December 2008. Federal recognition has allowed the tribe to enjoy a modicum of modern prosperity thanks to their land-based Paragon Casino Resort, one of Louisiana's largest, which attracts the multitudes with big-name entertainment in its 2,500-seat showroom and eight thousand-square-foot ballroom, lively gaming, spa, pool, championship golf course, extensive restaurants, and a huge five hundred-room hotel with an eight-story atrium recreating a Cajun village. The Tunica-Biloxi spring powwow affords an annual opportunity to celebrate the culture, with Native American dancers in colorful authentic regalia coming from across the country to participate.

ology and Native American traditions—demonstrations and classes on basketry, flintnapping, pottery, cornhusk doll making, and other relevant skills.

Today, the small reservation in Marksville houses members of the Tunica-Biloxi Tribe. In 1931, Chief Eli Barbry and a small group of tribal leaders went to Washington, D.C. to request federal recognition; however, their official status was not granted for fifty years, by which time their chief was Eli's grandson Earl. Earl Barbry, Sr., led the long, but eventually successful, struggle to have returned to the tribe their invaluable cultural and spiritual artifacts removed from Tunica burial sites across the river near the state penitentiary at Angola. Now these Indian and European artifacts are housed in the new two-story Tunica-Biloxi Indian Center and Museum on LA 1, which

Typical Native American dwelling hut from the Marksville culture, recreated in the Marksville State Historic Site Museum.

The Tunica-Biloxi spring powwow colorfully celebrates Native American culture.

Portal to the
Hill Country

Alexandria *and* Pineville

LA 1 rises through this region from the monotony of flat farm fields along the Red River to the rolling hills and piney woods, as the historic two-lane road travels within spitting distance of Louisiana's newest and most modern north-south superhighway, Interstate 49. Before reaching Alexandria, the state's crossroads community, travelers who are still hungry after leaving Louisiana's Cochon de Lait capital at Mansura would be well advised to take a short detour west to U.S. Highway 71 for lunch at Lecompte's famous Lea's Lunchroom, dubbed the state's pie capital and a Louisiana landmark since it was established in 1928. Still family owned and operated, Lea's bakes over sixty-five thousand pies a year, the crusts hand-rolled and the savory fillings made from secret family recipes.

Pineville and Alexandria developed on opposite banks of the Red River, so-called because of its reddish waters and red clay banks. The river originates at an elevation of five thousand feet in New Mexico on the Llano Estacado, flows east to form the border between Oklahoma and Texas, then crosses Louisiana to join the Atchafalaya and Mississippi rivers below the Three Rivers Wildlife Management Area midway down the state. Long blocked by logjams called the Great Raft, Louisiana's northern portion of the Red was not navigable until Capt. Henry Shreve cleared it in the 1830s, and a series of locks and dams built in the twentieth century re-opened navigation all the way north to the Shreveport area. For some time the Alexandria-Pineville area was the head of navigation on the Red, contributing to its importance as the trade center for the surrounding central Louisiana cotton culture, strategically situat-

ed as it was at the crossroads where El Camino Real from Texas and Old Mexico intersected the main north-south travel routes along the Mississippi River to and from New Orleans.

Captain Shreve docked the steamboat *Enterprise* at Alexandria in 1814, and within four years, the state legislature granted the town a charter. The area grew rapidly after Alexander Fulton, town founder, introduced the cotton gin to the area in 1800.

During the Civil War, Union Maj. Gen. Nathaniel P. Banks, commander of the Red River military expedition, passed through Alexandria marching toward Shreveport, coordinating his army troops with Rear Adm. David D. Porter's supporting naval forces on the river. The objectives of the Federal army's Red River Campaign involved capturing Shreveport, invading Texas, and preventing Mexico from supporting the Confederate cause. In addition, the Red River region contained large stores of cotton critical-

ly needed by the Union. But the Red River was extremely low in March 1864 as Porter assembled his fleet after capturing Fort De Russy near Marksville to the south, and, after being delayed waiting for the water levels to rise above the rapids at Alexandria, he was forced to leave many vessels behind on the push northwestward. The delay helped Confederate Gen. Richard Taylor reinforce and effectively deploy his smaller opposing forces, and he was able to defeat Banks' Union troops at the Battle of Mansfield near Shreveport.

Toward the end of April 1864, Banks withdrew his troops south to Alexandria, where the Red River once again proved a nearly insurmountable obstruction. The water level had fallen even lower, so that Admiral Porter's gunboats continually ran aground and at least one was sunk on the way downstream. At Alexandria the Red River at some points was only three feet deep; even the lightest of Porter's craft needed seven feet to pass, trapping thirty-five Federal gunboats above the two sets of exposed falls and rapids. Military engineer Lt. Col. Joseph Bailey came to the rescue with the outlandish proposal to build a dam to raise the water level and float the gunboats over the rapids.

The proposal met with universal ridicule, but Admiral Porter was desperate. Bailey had no formal engineering training but had learned hands-on skills of dam and bridge building in the lumber business on the Wisconsin frontier. He quickly set some three thousand troops to work day and night, chopping down trees, collecting stones and bricks, tearing down buildings for boards, the men often working up to their waists in water. On the north bank the dam was made of timber harvested along its shores, the logs laid with the current and branches interlocked. On the south bank, which was mostly cleared farmland, the dam was constructed of big cribs filled with stones, cotton gin machinery and any other heavy objects the troops could secure, the gap between the sides filled with scuttled barges.

The dam was built just above the lower rapids where the river was about 750 feet wide. Bailey's plan was to raise the water level behind the dam enough to float the gunboats over the upper rapids, then break the dam so the force of released water

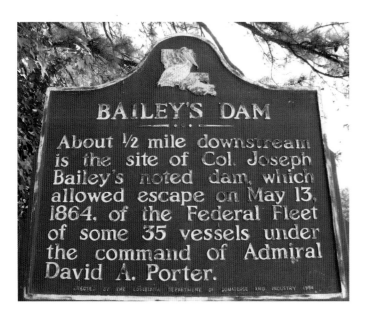

would carry the boats over the lower ones. It worked, though the main dam had to be augmented with a smaller one upriver. By May 12 the last of the Federal fleet shot through the rapids, grinding against the rocky river bottom and then shooting out into the safety of higher open waters as marching bands serenaded and applauding crowds assembled on the river banks.

Bailey's engineering skills would save the Union forces yet again as the expedition retreated south to the Atchafalaya River, where he fashioned a bridge out of twenty-four transport vessels held together by large timbers, with planks laid across the prows for the army to march safely across. As thanks, Bailey received a commemorative sword and was promoted to the rank of brigadier general. The archaeological remains of Bailey's Dam on the Red River, now submerged, are listed on the National Register of Historic Places as one of the greatest engineering feats of the Civil War, and a scenic overlook provides a view of their location from the Pineville side of the river. In addition, a state historic site near the O.K. Allen Bridge commemorates the remains of Fort Buhlow and Fort Randolph, earthenwork/moat fortifications constructed late in the war by the Confederates to make sure General Banks could not ascend the Red River again.

As the Union army troops retreated from Alexandria, the town was torched on Friday, May 13, 1864. Union soldiers' journals recorded horrific scenes of chaos, cows running bellowing through the streets, chickens flapping about with flaming feathers, crowds of terrified people running through unbearable heat carrying bundles soon dropped as they fled for their lives, and on the river levee thousands of assembled residents desperately wringing their hands beside little piles of what was left of their worldly possessions.

Consequently, there are few antebellum buildings in Alexandria. Fortunately, one of the few survivors is open to the public for daily tours. Kent Plantation House is considered the oldest standing

Bailey's Dam crossed the Red River at this site in 1864.

structure in central Louisiana, having been erected in 1800, five years before Alexander Fulton laid out the city of Alexandria. The Spanish land grant to French settler Pierre Baillio II dates from 1794, and his simple Creole home, raised atop brick piers over an open basement, was constructed of native materials—handhewn cypress, slave-made bricks, and between the timbers *bousillage* insulation, that useful muddle of mud, moss, and animal hair which in this red-dirt area has a distinct rosy hue. Baillio was the son of a French soldier stationed at the fort in Natchitoches, and he married Magdelaine Lacour of Pointe Coupée Parish.

In the 1840s, the second owner, Robert Hynson of Kent County, Maryland, named the plantation for his home region and added flanking one-room wings to each side of the house, showing later Greek Revival influence. Besides the dining room with swinging punka swishing away the insects and a formal ladies' parlor, the original house contained a single small bedroom for all the male children and an equally small bedroom for all the girls. Since the Baillios had fourteen children and the Hynsons ten, the additional wings were welcomed and used as a gentleman's study on one side and on the other a master bedroom filled not only with the parents' 1835 mahogany four-poster rolling-pin bed but also with children's cribs and cradles, a day bed, and a tin bathtub in which the entire family bathed sporadically.

The cash crop at Kent Plantation was white and brown cotton, with some indigo and just enough sugarcane grown for home use. Today the house is surrounded by four acres of typical dependencies, some of them (the milk house and carriage house) original and others moved to the site. Together these outbuildings provide a clear understanding of the operations of the early plantation complexes—tidy herb gardens and an outside kitchen with immense hearth and bread oven, an 1840s double slave cab-

Kent Plantation House

Milk house

in of *briquette-entre-poteaux* construction, a laundry room, an early 1800s dog-trot log barn filled with fascinating vintage agricultural implements and woodworking tools, a blacksmith shop where all the barrel staves and wagon wheels were made and horses were shod, the cotton house with a loom and spinning wheel, and the area's most complete sugar mill operation has a donkey-powered grinder and raised kettle train for cooking the juice to the point of crystalization in a graduated series of cast-iron pots called the *Batterie, Le Sirop, Le Flambeaux,* and *La Grande.* At Kent House, the annual Sugar Day in November recreates old-time sugarmaking amidst the revelry of a festival combining old-fashioned crafts, music, and food. Other living history demonstrations are presented periodically, featuring open-hearth cooking and blacksmithing, quilting, the use of herbs, and special children's activities.

In the Kent House gift shop are revolving exhibits highlighting significant influences on early plantation life, such as the scourge of yellow fever, an unwelcome summertime visitor in this land of hospitality, which filled family cemeteries like the one at Kent House with whole generations as the epidemics spread. Though most of Alexandria's early courthouse records were lost when Union soldiers

torched the town in 1864, the daily diaries of young Irish widow Honoria Griffin in the employ of Pierre Baillio's granddaughter, Mary Rose Emma Villain Prescott, are in the Kent House collection. Edited for publication by Carolyn Breedlove and entitled *A Glorious Day: The Journal of a Central Louisiana Governess, 1853-1854,* Griffin's chronicle records her own brush with yellow fever as it engulfed the region in 1853, quickly carrying off friends and relatives and requiring her to spend as much time sewing mourning clothing as tutoring the family children. Pierre Baillio's eldest son Sosthène Baillio, father of eight as well as Rapides Parish's representative in the state legislature and owner of the plantation that would become Flowerton, was only one of many victims. Griffin records several times in late summer that "the musquitoes [*sic*] are very bad," and on Thursday, October 6, "Mr. Baillio down with yellow fever. The day rather fine." By the following day she laments, "Mr. Baillio very ill, Dr. French came soon after breakfast, I eat no dinner. Hannah sent to know how Mr. Baillio was, brought word that he died about 4 o'C this morning. It was a great shock to us all. After breakfast I went up there, also Mrs. Barrett, found the house in confusion. Poor Mrs. Baillio to be pitied, Emily Anne lying very ill with

Carriage house

Kitchen

Slave cabin

Sugar Mill

Kettle train

The Louisiana History Museum shares Alexandria's original public library building with an extensive genealogical library.

fever." And by Sunday, October 9, Griffin writes, "I felt very ill indeed, all the symptoms of yellow fever were on me. About half an hour after I got settled in my bed, Rev. Mr. Temoin came in and heard my confession. I was very glad of the chance, as I thought I might die."

The Louisiana History Museum and the extensive Alexandria Genealogical Library share space in the old Alexandria public library building, which was set aside for public use on the original town square plat commissioned by Alexander Fulton in 1805. The museum has among its permanent displays exhibits on this dreaded disease and the early treatments that were nearly as deadly as the illness itself. In 1843, for example, Dr. D. Holt of New Orleans recommended the stricken be swathed in heavy blankets, feet immersed in hot water and mustard, and given hot tea filled with herbal laxatives for several days. It should be no surprise that the yellow fever exhibits also include plenty of black-bordered

funeral notices. It would be another half-century before Dr. Walter Reed and colleagues on the U.S. Army Commission on Yellow Fever identified mosquitoes as the culprits spreading the disease, a discovery of vital significance to the armed forces. During the Spanish-American War and U.S. occupation of Havana, for example, only 968 soldiers died of combat wounds, while five thousand died of disease, mostly yellow fever.

Other exhibits in the Louisiana History Museum feature prehistoric fossils, Indian artifacts, Revolutionary War and Louisiana Purchase displays, and antebellum fashions like the beaver hat worn by Montfort Wells at the famous race won by his thoroughbred horse Lecompte, for whom the town just south of Alexandria was named. The museum has military exhibits relating to Bailey's Dam, including a rusted anchor. One exhibit honors pilot John England, whose plane, low on fuel, would have crashed into his barracks without his selfless sacrifice; England Air Base was named for him. Another display pays tribute to Solomon Northup, a free man of color captured from New York state and sold into slavery at the area plantation of William Prince Ford. Once rescued, his experiences were chronicled in *Twelve Years A Slave*. There are vintage tools, medical and culinary displays, and political artifacts, including a bucket of Cottolene, the butter substitute hawked to rural housewives by a young Huey P. Long before he embarked on his public service career. While judging a Cottolene cookoff in 1911, he awarded the prize to Rose McConnell, and within a few years he would make her his wife. World War II mementoes in the Louisiana History Museum include V-mail and a large copy of the Japanese surrender document signed and sealed by Hirohito, "by the grace of Heaven, Emperor of Japan, seated on the throne occupied by the same dynasty changeless through ages eternal."

The Louisiana History Museum also has interesting displays on the Louisiana Maneuvers, called the dress rehearsal for World War II. As the United States prepared for World War II, the army chose central Louisiana as the site of the largest peacetime military maneuvers ever, with nearly half a million soldiers and a distinguished command staff including Eisenhower and Gen. George S. Patton coming together to devise the strategy and practice tactics that would eventually contribute to Allied victory. Gen. George C. Marshall, Army Chief of Staff, struggled to mechanize forces that still utilized World War I equipment—mounted cavalry, mule-drawn wagons, outdated rifles—but there was a need for field testing of new tanks and trucks as well as training for fresh troops in war games. The training

camps, airfields and other installations built for these maneuvers, which covered more than three thousand square miles in the summer of 1941, months before Pearl Harbor would precipitate America's inevitable entry into the conflict, would shape the course of history in this area.

The curator recalls entertaining local anecdotes from the era, such as the following chestnut: a young boy was thrown from a horse spooked by a new army vehicle called a Jeep transporting then-Col. Dwight D. Eisenhower, who was so solicitous of the youngster's well-being that he insisted upon driving him home. The boy's grateful mother shared with Ike some homemade ice cream and lemonade. When he asked if she made the treats often, she craftily replied that she could do so only when she had enough rationed sugar. From that day on, she received enough to entertain the congenial officer on many subsequent Sundays.

Several other museums in the area have exhibits on these massive maneuvers as well. One is located

The Louisiana History Museum has exhibits on the Louisiana Maneuvers prior to World War II.

Louisiana Maneuvers and Military Museum

to the west at Fort Polk Military Reservation, established in 1941, and still active as a Joint Readiness Training Center, and another one, called the Louisiana Maneuvers and Military Museum, can be found across the river in Pineville at Camp Beauregard. Named for Confederate general Pierre Gustave Toutant Beauregard, who ended a very short tenure as head of the United States Military Academy to join his native South and fire the opening salvos of the Civil War at Fort Sumter, the camp had its beginnings in 1917, when the War Department established an Army training facility near Alexandria. At the Camp Beauregard museum, two floors of a replica World War II-era barracks are filled with extensive exhibits on military history and the Louisiana Maneuvers, including displays of vintage uniforms from the Revolutionary War and beyond, airplanes,

artifacts, weaponry and equipment; even a typical

Hotel Bentley

latrine is on display to give visitors a real feel for service life.

In Alexandria, the wonderfully elaborate Hotel Bentley overlooking the Red River served as headquarters for many of the top-ranked military leaders participating in the Louisiana Maneuvers; it has gone through several reincarnations in recent years.

The vast England Air Force Base, though closed in 1992, remains a reminder of the importance of the military presence here. It retains present-day viability in its beautifully resurrected state as England Industrial Air Park, its landscaped entrance graced with vintage aircraft mounted as if in flight. Its present tenants include a boutique hotel, golf course, fine restaurant, and municipal airport.

In Alexandria's vibrant downtown historic and cultural district along the Red River are several interesting museums, including the Alexandria Museum of Art in the picturesque Renaissance Revival Rapides Bank Building, circa 1898. Located on the entire 900 block of Main Street, the museum contains changing gallery exhibits of fine art and Louisiana folk art and fabulous views of the river from its upper stories.

Alexandria Museum of Art

Arna Bontemps African American Museum

The Arna Bontemps African American Museum and Cultural Arts Center preserves the restored 1890s birthplace of Arna Bontemps, a writer, educator, and librarian who played a major role in the Harlem Renaissance, along with Langston Hughes, W. E. B. DuBois, Zora Neale Hurston, Countee Cullen, and other emerging literary figures. For the first time, this movement acknowledged and introduced to the world outstanding young black talent in jazz, theater, and literature. Bontemps' award-winning body of work included dozens of books, biographies, plays, and poems that dealt with black life and culture. His children's literature utilized the rich rhythms and themes of African American folk culture; he also edited a number of anthologies on black literature. It opened in 1992, nine decades after Bontemps' birth, and was the state's first African American museum.

The Alexandria Zoological Park, founded in 1926, is called Central Louisiana's number one tourist attraction, with more than six hundred animals scattered across thirty-three well-designed and landscaped acres crisscrossed by wooden boardwalks, including an award-winning Louisiana habitat area. The zoo is especially child-friendly, with a popular train ride and low-level fencing or clear enclosures so pint-sized visitors can get nose-to-nose with the colorful exotic birds and wild animals from Africa, Asia, Australia, and the Americas.

Across the river in Pineville, the Old Town Hall Museum is housed in the 1935 brick town hall and showcases typical municipal governmental offices, courtroom and police station, the old holding cell and courtroom, even a bright red vintage fire truck garaged underneath.

Pineville's Old Town Hall Museum

Kisatchie National Forest

Pineville is the headquarters for Louisiana's only national forest, which is managed by the United States Forest Service. It consists of some six hundred thousand acres, nearly one thousand square miles, spread across central and northern Louisiana in six geographically separate units in seven different parishes, with scenic vistas, waterfalls, dozens of miles of multiple-use trails and wilderness hiking trails, overnight camping facilities and plenty of other recreational opportunities. The national forest was established in 1929, beginning the reforestation of thousands of cutover acres in central Louisiana, where the lumber industry had tremendous economic impact.

The Longleaf Trail Scenic Byway, accessed via the Derry exit from LA 1, is considered one of the

Little Bayou Pierre cascade in Kisatchie National Forest

One of the scenic overlooks in the Red Dirt District of Kisatchie National Forest, looking toward LA 1.

RED COCKADED WOODPECKER
NEST TREES

PRESERVE THESE TREES

These aged pines serve as nesting trees for the RED COCKADED WOODPECKER - a bird becoming scarce. Because of heart rot, such trees are unsuitable for timber, but are in great demand by this bird. Help us protect these trees so we can keep this woodpecker.

state's most scenic drives, with rugged terrain ranging in elevation from 120 to 400 feet above sea level. This seventeen-mile drive follows a high ridge through the hills, with views and vistas extending more than twenty miles. The Military Road section of the trail was used by troops during the Civil War. Longleaf Vista provides scenic views of mesas, buttes, and sandstone outcroppings for which this area is noted, while the Caroline Dormon Hiking and Horse Trail extends twelve miles through wildflower meadows and longleaf pines in memory of one of the forest's great promoters and preservers. The first woman employed in forestry in the United States, Dormon was an early conservationist and naturalist who has come to be known as the "Mother of Kisatchie." The Longleaf Trail Byway, which skirts the Kisatchie Hills Wilderness, featuring rugged terrain with steep slopes and unusual topography, is immensely popular with hikers. Formed mil-

lions of years ago, the Kisatchie Hills have been also called the Little Grand Canyon.

Several units of Kisatchie National Forest have been designated Louisiana Important Bird Areas by the National Audubon Society, and along the Longleaf Trail one may see a number of areas important in the reestablishment and improvement of prime habitat area for both quail and for the endangered red-cockaded woodpeckers, who nest in over-mature pines left behind by loggers due to disease, deformity, or small size. Many of these nesting trees have been marked along the Longleaf Trail as it passes through part of the 38,450-acre National Red Dirt Wildlife Management Preserve, where the U.S. Forest Service shares oversight duties with the Louisiana Department of Wildlife and Fisheries.

Kisatchie Bayou is included in the Louisiana Natural and Scenic Stream System to protect its natural beauty. Kisatchie is the Indian word for "cane coun-

The Kisatchie Bayou flows through Kisatchie National Forest.

try," so called because of the patches of cane along the bayou's banks. Today it is one of the most popular camping and picnicking spots in the forest. The clear bayou waters rush over boulders in a series of rapids more reminiscent of Yosemite and other western parks than Louisiana landscapes, and there are actually real waterfalls along Little Bayou Pierre and Kisatchie Bayou. Along the Longleaf Trail, camping with facilities is featured at Kisatchie Bayou Recreation Area and at Dogwood, while other sites offer more primitive camping.

Besides the Longleaf Trail Scenic Byway, Kisatchie National Forest has a number of other popular trails in different sections near the Alexandria-Pineville area. The twenty-five-mile Wild Azalea Trail extends from bottomlands hardwood forests into upland piney woods brightened by the springtime blooms of azaleas and wild dogwoods, and has been designated as a National Recreation Trail. Kincaid and Valentine Lake Recreation Complexes offer swimming, boating, biking, fishing, hunting, camping, and hiking. Saline Bayou National Scenic River offers canoeing along cypress bayou waters. Gum Springs Horse Trail has hiking and horseback riding, and even trails for covered wagons.

Statue dedicated to men who served in the Civilian Conservation Corps in Louisiana during the Great Depression.

Creole Country

Along this stretch of LA 1 the waving stalks of sugarcane have given way to snowy cotton in flat fields so vast they seem to stretch unbroken to the horizon. Supplanting earlier cash crops of indigo and tobacco along the Cane and Red rivers, cotton assumed the ascendancy for most of the nineteenth century, and for the planters and slaves or sharecroppers, life ebbed and flowed with the cotton crop. After the fields were prepared in late winter and early spring, they were plowed with mules, and the crop was planted in March and April. By June and July, the plants were covered in blooms, first creamy, then pink, then deepening to purple, blooms of great beauty; after all, this plant is a member of the hibiscus family. By late summer, the blooms wilted into bolls that darkened from green to brown as they dried and opened to reveal the fluffy white cotton inside. Late August, September, and October were the prime harvest months, with the cotton picking going on for three or four long and weary months when it was done by hand, the fieldworkers dragging long sacks behind them as they moved through the rows from daylight to dark. Adult fieldhands

were expected to pick at least two hundred pounds of cotton every day, and children were often drafted for picking as well. Then the process of ginning and baling and shipping completed the cycle that would begin all over again all too soon.

In 1793, the introduction of Eli Whitney's cotton gin with its spike teeth, later modernized with the use of saw blades, encouraged the rapid rise of the cotton culture by helping to combat the main problem with cotton—its seeds. Each cotton boll could have as many as twenty-eight tightly imbedded seeds, the removal of which by hand was time consuming and costly, but an absolute necessity before the lint could be cleaned and compressed into bales and shipped off to mills to answer the voracious demands of the burgeoning textile age. The gins and presses were first mule-powered, then steam-powered, with capacity and efficiency increasing accordingly. By 1860, some two-thirds of all cotton grown in America was produced east of the Mississippi as the cotton empire expanded westward from depleted East Coast lands through the rich Mississippi delta,

Orderly rows of a pecan orchard

and nowhere was there richer land than along Louisiana's rivers, including the Red and Cane.

Huge acreages of cotton are still planted along here, in spite of some lean years occasioned by the invasion of the boll weevil, combined with labor shortages and changing economic situations. Today, some of the former cotton plantation lands are crisscrossed by the orderly rows of extensive pecan orchards. Most of the pecans grown in the United States—some 80 percent of the world's pecan crop—are produced here in the South's Pecan Belt.

Historic Little Eva Plantation is said to have had some connection to author Harriet Beecher Stowe's antislavery novel *Uncle Tom's Cabin*; Stowe visited the area in the 1840s, and the slave Tom, purchased

in the book by a Louisiana plantation owner, saves his master's small devout daughter, the beloved Little Eva, from drowning in the Mississippi River. Some versions of local lore point to an antebellum area landowner who mistreated his slaves as the inspiration for the book's cruel Simon Legree, and some have even implied the existence of actual burial sites of Uncle Tom and his master, though Stowe insisted her characters were fictional composites drawn from many influences. Today, the plantation has thousands of pecan trees, with each managed acre capable of producing up to one thousand pounds. Most years, the plantation stores opposite each other on both sides of LA 1 permit autumn travelers to purchase fresh-picked samples of this rich har-

Railroad depot moved from Natchez, La.

vest, offering everything from plain natural pecans to gourmet flavors—spiced or glazed, chocolate or amaretto covered, roasted or honey toasted, in patties, pralines, or brittle. In addition, pecans can be ordered online and shipped year-round in an assortment of tins and gift baskets. On one side of the highway, the big red barn pecan outlet cozies up to the historic railroad depot moved down the road from Natchez, Louisiana.

Besides its repeated associations with *Uncle Tom's Cabin*, Little Eva Plantation was the birthplace of Clementine Hunter, whose life began as a slave and ended on Melrose Plantation as a nationally acclaimed folk artist. Cloutierville was also the home of another creative genius, author Kate Chopin, who is considered one of nineteenth-century America's most important writers. Born in St. Louis in 1851, she married at the age of nineteen a Louisiana French Creole named Oscar Chopin. Chopin's failure as a cotton factor in New Orleans sent the family back to tiny Cloutierville, where he ran a general store and raised crops on the family plantations while his young wife raised eyebrows by smoking, flirt-

ing shamelessly, and exhibiting other fast "Yankee" mannerisms frowned upon by proper small-town Southern society. She also was an astute observer of the culture and customs surrounding her, both in the Crescent City and along the Cane. When Oscar Chopin died in 1882, his widow returned to St. Louis and supported her six young children by penning stories that immortalized early Louisiana life and scandalized straight-laced Victorian society by exposing the repressed longings of wives like the heroine of *The Awakening*, to whom freedom could come only in the welcomed embrace of the windswept waves off Grand Isle. Her short stories of colorful characters were first published in contemporary periodicals like *Atlantic Monthly* and *Harper's Young People*. Dozens were later collected in *Bayou Folk* and *A Night in Acadie*, in which the vagaries and vicissitudes of life and love in early Louisiana meander along as many unexpected twists and turns as the old Cane River itself and in which the eyes of wistful women smolder with "fires which would never flame."

What became known as the Kate Chopin House

and Bayou Folk Museum in Cloutierville was built around 1809 by town founder Alexis Cloutier. Cloutier cleared the canebreaks along the Cane River to establish a plantation and was said to have amassed a fortune without ever learning to read or write. His social skills seem to have been lacking as well, for his second wife divorced him within just three months of marriage after he allegedly became abusive when she refused to wash his feet.

Incorporated in 1822, the town of Cloutierville served as the supply center for the nearby plantations and lumber industry, providing banks, barbershops, medical offices, a cotton gin, general stores, racetrack, even an opera house. Alexis Cloutier hoped to establish Cloutierville as the new parish seat, but when his proposal to divide Natchitoches Parish was rejected, he sold his holdings and moved to Little Eva Plantation. Cloutierville also experienced a decline as the mechanization of farming operations and the decrease in large-scale logging caused a significant

depopulation in the surrounding area. Today the lazy little town, its lawns sloping down to the river-banks, has a decidedly relaxed air, with goats grazing in front yards right on the main street and some of the historic buildings caving in from neglect. In *Bayou Folk*, which was first published in 1894, Kate Chopin called Cloutierville a little French village consisting simply of two long rows of very old frame houses facing each other closely across a dusty road-way, and for the most part, so it remains today.

It was at a sheriff's sale that Oscar Chopin bought the Kate Chopin House in 1879. A two-story raised cottage with a ground floor of bricks and *bousillage*, it had upper-level living quarters with flooring of five-inch heart pine. Most recently owned by the Association for the Preservation of Historic Natchitoches, the property included an early log blacksmith shop and a doctor's office, but in a fate all too common to unoccupied historic structures, the main house burned in the fall of 2008.

Kate Chopin House prior to destruction by fire

Cane River

Early settlement and development patterns followed the water courses, the rivers and bayous which were the main means of transportation for immigrating settlers and their supplies and for transshipment of their trade goods and produce to external markets. But rivers can be fickle friends at best. They overflow and enrich the soil, building up high natural levees that make perfect homesites and fertilizing flat alluvial bottomlands perfect for planting cash crops. But sometimes those meandering rivers tire of rounding endless curves and take a shortcut, stranding communities high and dry. The Red River did this in the early 1800s, partly due to the obstruction of the Great Raft—the more than 160-mile logjam that restricted navigation upriver above Natchitoches.

Without its river flowing through it, Natchitoches, although still along busy overland trade routes and a gateway to the West, suddenly found itself no longer an important riverport. But the river's abandonment just might have been a blessing in disguise. The thirty-five-mile long curve of waterway that was cut off when the Red River in the 1830s switched its main channel five miles east was dammed to make lovely languid Cane River Lake, and the history and heritage that developed along the fertile banks of this oxbow lake engender one of the most unique cultures in the entire country. This is Cane River Creole country, so rich in preserved treasures that it boasts a comprehensive National Heritage Area, several National Historic Parks, six National Historic Landmarks, an in-town National Historic Landmark District, and a huge number of National Register structures bespeaking a way of life like no other. It goes without saying that the area abounds in dedicated individual preservationists and hard-working local and national organizations determined to interpret and protect the area's past to

enhance its present.

One of the most historic sections of Louisiana, the Cane River area in the very early eighteenth century attracted French and Spanish trappers, traders and soldiers, who established colonial military and trade outposts in these lands of the Natchitoches band of Caddo Indians. As the Europeans settled down and began to clear the canebrakes along the riverbanks to establish small farms and plantations, cultivating first indigo and tobacco and then cotton, African slaves were imported to work the fields. As the prospects of agricultural success brightened, Anglo-Americans moved in from the East Coast and the Mississippi Valley after the Louisiana Purchase of 1803, and there were also *gens de couleur libres*, free persons of color, many of them highly skilled artisans like the blacksmiths whose gracefully curved iron crosses mark many of the earliest graves. Each nationality made its contribution to the history of the area, and in the lonely wilderness outposts, some unusual partnerships were struck; the white Creoles born in this country of French and Spanish descent were soon joined by remarkable generations of Creoles of color whose ancestry, like the heritage of the Cane River area itself, harmoniously blended French, Spanish, Indian, and African blood and traditions.

The best introduction to eighteenth-century plantation life experienced by the French colonialists in the area is provided by the Cane River Creole National Historical Park, which was established by the federal government in 1994 in recognition of the region's significance as a unique cultural landscape, along with the thirty-five-mile-long Cane River National Heritage Area. Following the course of the Cane just to the east of LA 1 along Highways 119, 484, and 494, the park was incorporated into the National Park System in order to preserve more than sixty historic structures and thousands

Cane River

Two of the eight rare brick slave cabins on Magnolia Plantation

of artifacts on two significant properties, Oakland and Magnolia plantations, between Cloutierville and Natchitoches. The Cane River Creole National Historical Park brochure provides perhaps the most understandable description of the unique early society that developed in this unusual area, calling it "an open crossroads world where cultural exchanges and marital unions among French, Spanish, French Canadian, African and American Indian cultures were producing a dynamic frontier society with a distinctive French accent."

The Magnolia Unit of Cane River Creole National Park includes the plantation's agricultural and industrial facilities, but not the large main house, which was burned by Union forces during the Civil War and then rebuilt by the Hertzog family in 1896; today the structure remains a private family residence. Accessible to visitors are the plantation store, slave hospital/overseer's house, blacksmith shop, 1840 *pigeonnier*, and cotton gin where workers fed

tons of cotton fiber into the steam-powered gin and pressed it into bales weighing between four hundred and five hundred pounds apiece in the mule- or, later, steam-powered presses. The 11x30-foot wooden screw-type horse-powered cotton press, dating from 1835, is considered the last one remaining in its original location in the country. In the fields are eight rare brick single and double pen slave quarters, all that are left of an original seventy cabins. As early as 1753, Jean-Baptiste LeComte received land grants along the river here which his son Ambroise and descendants (two of Ambroise's daughters married two Hertzog brothers) expanded significantly to include over 7,500 acres worked by more than 275 slaves; the present Magnolia Plantation, a National Bicentennial Farm, sits on 960 arpents acquired by the LeComtes from Gasparite LaCour.

The Oakland Plantation Unit of the park was originally a land grant to Jean Pierre Phillippe Prud'homme, a soldier born in France and stationed

Oakland Plantation house, approached from the Cane River through an avenue of live oaks

Flowerbeds bordered by upturned wine bottles at Oakland

in the French colony of Louisiana, where he began farming in 1785. By 1789, he had acquired land-grant property upon which his grandson Jean Pierre Emmanuel Prud'homme built a raised Creole cottage of cypress and *bousillage* in 1821. The plantation was originally called Bermuda. At the beginning of the Civil War, Emmanuel's son Pierre Phanor Prud'homme owned ten plantations and more than one thousand slaves to work his cotton fields, many of whom stayed on after the war to labor as sharecroppers or tenant farmers. Eight generations of the Prud'homme family worked this land, and they were considered the first family west of the Mississippi to farm cotton on such a large scale. Today, thanks to their good stewardship, the main house at Oakland is flanked by a large number of original outbuildings, including the plantation store/post of-fice and twenty-seven other dependencies, providing a colorful and comprehensive picture of plantation life from 1785 to 1960, just before mechanization led to an out-migration of rural farm workers. A magnificent alley of live oaks planted around 1825 approaches the front of the Oakland house from the Cane, providing shade and shelter and drafting cool breezes from the river, and the antebellum flower-beds around the front stairs are bordered with color-ful upturned wine bottles. Visitors to Oakland tour the main house and outbuildings. Other early nine-teenth-century plantation residences in the area, pri-vately owned and not generally accessible to visitors, include Oaklawn, Cherokee, and Beau Fort planta-tions, all listed on the National Register of Historic Places.

Along the Cane River between Magnolia and

147

Beau Fort Plantation

Oakland is Melrose, a National Historic Landmark carefully preserved under the auspices of the Association for the Preservation of Historic Natchitoches. Here visitors gain an understanding of Cane River Creole culture through the superbly simple paintings of Clementine Hunter, who progressed from slave to laundress to big-house cook to—in her older years—world-famous primitive painter. Hunter recorded life as she saw it on everything she could get her hands on: bottles, coffee pots, shingles, window shades, flatirons, walls, and sometimes even canvas. She preserved cotton picking, church suppers, riverside baptisms, flying angels (a couple of them flamboyantly red instead of pristine white, because the artist said there were bad angels too!), laundry day, and all the facets of plantation life in living color. In Hunter's images strong women towered over teeny tiny men, symbolic of the esteem (or lack thereof) in which the artist held her various subjects.

And indeed, the Cane River Creole story is the story of strong women of courage at Melrose Plantation, beginning with the remarkable Marie Thérèse CoinCoin, born a slave in 1742 in the household

Clementine Hunter

Hunter's rendition of wash day

of Louis Juchereau de St. Denis, first commandant of the French post at Natchitoches. After producing four children with a slave consort, she was purchased by French entrepreneur Claude Thomas Pierre Metoyer, by whom she would have ten more children. After he freed her and some of their children, CoinCoin worked furiously to earn funds to purchase the freedom of her other offspring. Metoyer deeded to her a small piece of property. Between 1794 and 1803, she and

The African House is reminiscent of Congo thatch-roofed huts.

her sons applied for and received a number of other land grants; Melrose was recorded in the name of her son Louis Metoyer. The lands were laboriously cleared to raise crops, and the first dwelling on Melrose Plantation, Yucca House, was built in 1796 of virgin cypress beams and *bousillage* insulation made of a mixture of mud, moss, and deer hair. The unusual African House, strangely reminiscent of Congo thatch-roofed huts, was erected around 1800 for use as storehouse and slave jail. Today the upper walls of the African House are covered with Hunter's colorful murals. The impressive Melrose Big House dates from 1833 and is a typical raised Creole plantation structure. Its lower floor built of brick and upper living quarters of wood, Melrose is now shaded by immense live oaks.

Clementine Hunter covered the upper walls of the African House with colorful murals of plantation life.

Melrose Plantation

Fine furnishings and family portraits grace the interior of Melrose.

The Badin-Roque House is a typical *bousillage* frontier dwelling.

The Metoyer family grew and prospered, with succeeding generations branching out across the Isle Brevelle, that narrow strip of land stranded between several early channels of the Red River. The dirt-floored Badin-Roque House across the waterway from Melrose has been preserved as a typical *bousillage* frontier dwelling, one of a few in the country in the style called *poteaux-en-terre*, its handhewn cypress posts set directly in the ground. Overlooking the water nearby is St. Augustine Catholic Church. In 1803, when CoinCoin's devout eldest son Nicholas Augustin Metoyer and his brother Louis founded this church, it was considered the first Roman Catholic church established by and for parishioners of color in the country, and it would become the only known church with members predominantly of color to sponsor a mission, St. Charles Chapel just up the river, for a white congregation.

Melrose was sold and its contents were auctioned in 1970, long after the Metoyers had lost it to white ownership in the tough economic times of the 1840s. The huge and valuable 1830 portrait of family patriarch Augustin, who rose from slavery to respectable prosperity as a free planter and community leader, was put on the block. The determined priest of St. Augustine, Father Rosso, joined by a group of church members whom he introduced individually as Metoyer descendants, bid on the portrait all the funds he had been able to raise, just $2,000. The auctioneer tried to up the ante, but there were no other bids from the sympathetic crowd, and the portrait of founder Augustin assumed its rightful place in the church atrium where it hangs today. When he died in 1856, his large white tomb was placed directly behind his church, its inscription, like many others around it, in French. After two centuries, St.

Little St. Charles Chapel, a mission sponsored by St. Augustine Church

Augustine Church remains the spiritual and social hub of the Isle Brevelle community. The church gained national fame as the setting for the wedding in the movie *Steel Magnolias*, and the history of the remarkable CoinCoin and her descendants forms the basis for a growing body of literature, both fact and fiction.

Hypolite and Henry Hertzog purchased Melrose from the Metoyers, and they in turn lost it in the desperate years after the Civil War. In 1884, Joseph Henry acquired the property, which became home around the turn of the twentieth century to John Hampton and Cammie Garrett Henry. "Miss Cammie," an avid preservationist, enthusiastic gardener and great patron of the arts who bustled about in starched white shirtwaists and long black wool skirts as seen displayed upon her four-poster bed even to-

day, added flanking *garçonnières* and a kitchen wing to the house. She was a weaver who resurrected local crafts, and her stone-chimneyed weaving house displays early looms. She used her peaceful plantation setting to foster creativity by hosting writers and artists like Erskine Caldwell, Alexander Woolcott, William Faulkner, John Steinbeck, Gwen Bristow, Harnett Kane, and Lyle Saxon, gathering them at dinner each night to report on their daily progress. One writer, François Mignon, arrived for a six-week visit and stayed thirty-two years. It was during this period that an appreciation emerged for the talents of Clementine Hunter, one-time Melrose cook. It is gratifying that even today some of the staff interpreting for visitors the unique micro-culture surrounding Melrose trace their ancestry directly to the legendary CoinCoin and her Metoyer offspring.

St. Augustine Catholic Church

155

Natchitoches

Natchitoches is the oldest permanent European settlement in the vast Louisiana Purchase. Today, its European heritage is very much alive, and a state historic site recreates that first French footprint, Fort St. Jean-Baptiste de Natchitoches, which had its beginnings near the site of a Natchitoches Indian village. This earliest garrisoned post was established to control Spanish incursions from the province of Texas into French Louisiana and to protect an area increasingly vital as a trade center, with the Native American tribes of the Caddo Confederacies facilitating commerce and communication among early pioneers both French and Spanish. Conversely, just fifteen miles to the west, the Spanish constructed their own presidio in the 1700s to protect Texas from the French, and its remains are preserved as Los Adaes State Historic Site. This was the first capital of Spanish Texas, and the settlement established the border between Mexico and Louisiana. Nearby is the Adai Caddo Historic Village at Robeline, complete with tepees and buffalo herd, preserving the traditions of another branch of the Caddo Confed-

Bust of Louis Juchereau de St. Denis

eracies. The territory of the Adai extended from the Red River west across the Sabine River, and these Native American cowboys excelled in rounding up wild mustangs and cattle to trade with other tribes as well as early French and Spanish settlers.

The first commandant of Fort St. Jean-Baptiste de Natchitoches was Louis Juchereau de St. Denis, French Canadian relative of Iberville, who diplomatically guided the growth of the region for several decades; today, his bust presides over the riverfront near the tourist information center in Natchitoches. In the 1970s, a replica of his fort was constructed by the state with eighteenth-century tools and techniques, using detailed drawings made in the 1730s by French engineer-in-chief Ignace François Broutin, complete with protective double palisade of pointed poles surrounding barracks, warehouse, powder magazine, guardhouse, church, and other crude but functional log facilities. Costumed interpreters, living-history demonstrations, and an interesting visi-

Fort St. Jean-Baptiste de Natchitoches State Historic Site replicates early settlement in the region.

Church Street in the National Historic Landmark District

tor center make this colonial outpost come alive for visitors to the state historic site today.

Along the banks of this wonderful river/lake, the Cane, north of the Creole plantation country, rise the picturesque structures of the National Historic Landmark District in Natchitoches, a thirty-three-block area comprising only one of two such districts in the state, the other being the Vieux Carré in New Orleans, to which this district bears striking similarities. This is surely one of the loveliest downtown areas of the state, its bricked main street, Front Street, overlooking the river from atop the levee, its picturesque Victorian lampposts hung with immense baskets of colorful blooms and its tidy walkways lined with inviting benches. Natchitoches has gained recognition as a Great American Main Street, one of the National Trust's Dozen Distinctive Destinations, a Preserve America Community, and, of course, the setting for the movie *Steel Magnolias*. Since its inception in 1926, its famous Festival of Lights has attracted thousands to admire the brilliant holiday displays along the riverside from mid-November until early January, featuring more than three hundred thousand Christmas bulbs and over one hundred riverbank set pieces, plus fireworks, parades, arts and crafts, musical entertainment, horse-drawn carriage tours, river cruises, and plenty of food. Other popular annual events include the Natchitoches-

Victorian lampposts hung with colorful flower baskets brighten historic Front Street.

Kaffie-Frederick Store

NSU Folk Festival showcasing the area's culinary, handicraft and musical heritage, periodic pilgrimage tours of historic homes, lively music festivals, and the Meat Pie Festival.

Historic double-galleried commercial structures line Front Street, many with upstairs living lofts, first-floor restaurants, upscale shops, and a wonderfully eclectic bookstore that usually has a gigantic cat dozing in its storefront window and others snoozing on the shelves inside. A couple of these Front Street structures retain carriage drives from the street to rear courtyards, and many feature fine cast-iron grillwork balconies. The big brick Kaffie-Frederick Store, in the present location since the 1890s, was opened for business in 1863 by Jewish immigrants from Prussia and is called the oldest continuously operated hardware store in the country. Across the river, homes overlooking the lake and lining oak-shaded boulevards present a fascinating mixture of Queen Anne and Victorian architecture with Creole cottages, many with manicured lawns sloping down to boathouses and piers along the waterway. Sitting

Roselawn is an example of colorful Queen Anne architecture.

Roque House sits right on the river bank.

below Front Street, on the river level where visitors can catch cablecar city tours, is the beautifully landscaped 1796 Roque House, built of handhewn timbers and *bousillage* by a free man of color. An oversized shingled roof forms a gallery around the home. Until 1941, Roque House was occupied by Mme. Marie Philomène Metoyer Roque, daughter of Augustin Metoyer, patriarch of the Cane River Creoles of color on Isle Brevelle.

The home of Northwestern State University, established in 1884 to train the state's teachers, Natchitoches is as well known for its huge assortment of colorful bed & breakfasts as it is for its signature dish, the spicy Natchitoches meat pie, best sampled at venerable Lasyone's Restaurant on 2nd Street in the old Masonic Lodge, a block up from the river. Also on 2nd Street is the huge Church of the Immaculate Conception, the spiritual center of the parish dating back to the early eighteenth century, when the Apostle of Texas, Venerable Antonio Margil de Jésus, walked fifteen miles from the Spanish mission at Los Adaes to celebrate mass for the French garrison at Fort St. Jean-Baptiste each Sunday.

Church of the Immaculate Conception

OLD COURTHOUSE MUSEUM

Across the street from the church is the big brick Romanesque Old Courthouse Museum with its eye-catching tower, that was built in 1896 and is now a branch of the Louisiana State Museum. Among its simple exhibits are a series of miniature recreations of early Creole French concessions and cotton plantations showing in great if miniscule detail the daily life on these early properties, the miniature men operating *passe-partout* crosscut saws to hew timbers for building, the tiny slaves attending to their duties in the quarters behind the big house, the river steamboats pausing at the plantation landing, where an ant-sized fisherman lounges with his cane pole.

Natchitoches National Fish Hatchery

At the southern entrance to Natchitoches on LA 1 is the Natchitoches National Fish Hatchery. Administered by the U.S. Fish and Wildlife Service, the hatchery spawns, hatches, and raises various sport and endangered fish species—largemouth and striped bass, bluegill, channel cat, paddlefish, and pallid sturgeon, as well as alligator snapping turtles and Louisiana pearlshell mussels. It also has an interesting sixteen-tank aquarium with live warm-water fish, alligators, and a rare albino snapping turtle. Since its beginnings in 1931, the hatchery has stocked nearly 165 million fingerlings. There are also interesting historic displays here, since the hatchery sits on land occupied as early as the fifteenth century by Native American members of the Caddo Nation, and hundreds of pottery shards, beads, metal objects, and other artifacts have been excavated on the site. Archeological evidence compiled during a 1930s study spearheaded by the Smithsonian suggested that this was the location of the Natchitoches Caddo village visited by Henri de Tonti ca. 1690. By the mid-1800s, the Caddo had been removed to reservations in the Oklahoma Territory, but enduring cultural traditions of the tribe, like their alligator dance, bespeak an origin much closer to Louisiana's waterways than the Dust Bowl.

Grand Ecore

Above Natchitoches, slightly east of LA 1 on LA 6, is the Grand Ecore Visitor Center atop a high bluff overlooking a horseshoe bend in the Red River, offering spectacular views from its patio and a shady gazebo eighty feet above the water. Exhibits interpret the natural and cultural history of the region, with detailed explanations of the riverscape and its importance to settlement and trade for more than three centuries. The role of the Corps of Engineers in developing, preserving, and enhancing the water resources of the region is featured in displays explaining the history of navigation on the river. Through a series of locks and dams, navigation has been made possible for 236 miles from Shreveport to the Mississippi River along what is called the J. Bennett Johnston Waterway project. Grand Ecore itself began as a Spanish land grant to Athanase de Mézières, son-in-law of the founder of Natchitoches, and the settlement became a thriving antebellum riverport, with stagecoaches and steamboats loaded with cotton stopping over at the "Great Bluff." Devastated by a yellow fever epidemic in the 1850s and torched by Union troops for having served as a Confederate outpost during the Red River Campaign in the Civil War, Grand Ecore never recovered.

Grand Ecore Visitor Center, atop a high bluff, offers spectacular views of a horseshoe bend in the Red River.

Powhatan

Named for the Virginia Indian chief who is best known as the father of Pocahontas, Powhatan today is the site of an Alligator Park sprawling over five acres along Bayou Pierre. The park, sitting amidst fertile farm fields, features hundreds of gators visitors can watch from covered protected walkways or even hold, alligator feeding shows featuring thousand-pound gators leaping out of the water for treats, reptile habitat, bird sanctuary with walk-in aviary, feeding zoo with pygmy goats and raccoons and other small animals, plus music and "Cajun" food, including lots of alligator dishes. The park is open daily late spring through summer and weekends only until mid-fall. It is closed during the winter when alligators are not very active. Watch the roadside for the big ol' alligator that in a prior life must have been a school bus.

Another eye-catching yellow landmark along LA 1 is the cheerfully sunny Powhatan railroad depot, complete with water tank, RR crossing sign, and old baggage carts, reclaimed by local historian "Mr. Buddy" Maggio to house his ever-increasing collection of local memorabilia. The T&P Railroad stopped at old lumber towns, and Mr. Buddy has lovingly salvaged the depot, the Atkins Store, and parts of another late nineteenth-century local country store. On April 12, 1864, this was the site of the Battle of Blair's Landing during the Red River Campaign of the Civil War, where Confederate Brig. Gen. Tom Green was killed by a direct hit

Farm fields surrounding the Alligator Park bustle with tractors and cultivators.

The bright yellow Powhatan railroad depot houses a museum of local memorabilia.

from a mortar shell fired from the USS *Osage.* Mr. Buddy shows off a model of the battle during which Union gunboats fired point blank into Green's Louisiana artillery and Texas cavalry who had recently routed the Yankees at Mansfield and Pleasant Hill. That the Confederates fired back just as fiercely was verified by testimony that after the battle the USS *Black Hawk* looked as if pitted by smallpox, without a single place six inches square not perforated by a bullet. Besides a number of Civil War artifacts, logs embedded with minie balls, and other exhibits, the depot, which had "colored" and "white" waiting rooms typical of the times and a rear country store with beaded-board wainscoting and glass showcases, provides a picture of turn-of-the-century life along this stretch of the Red River and LA 1, where the orderly pecan orchards of Natchitoches Parish give way to the picturesque rolling pasturelands of cattle country in Red River Parish.

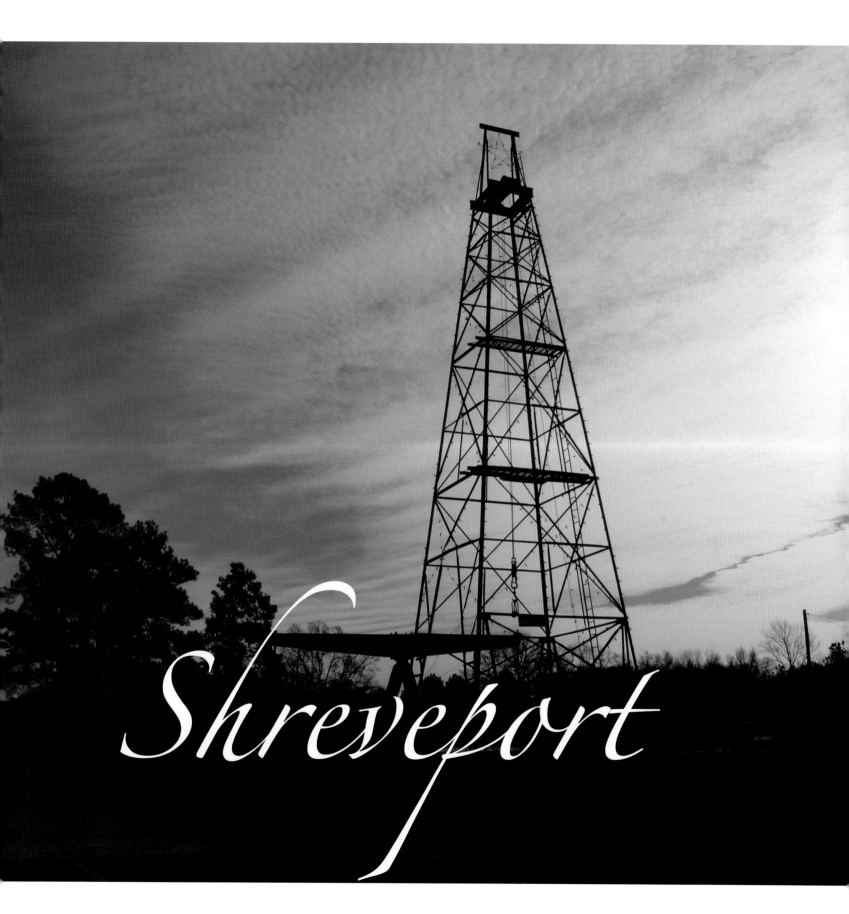

Caspiana

The journey along LA 1 began with bountiful harvests of fresh gulf and bayou seafood and passed through the abundance of fertile sugarcane, then cotton fields. Now, as we approach the culmination of our statewide passage, we notice more and more weather-beaten cabins, abandoned and desolate beneath a single shade tree in the midst of uncultivated fields. Old country stores like that of C.M. Hutchinson & Son, once congenial centers of community life, lapse into langorous states of decay beside the railroad tracks. Before a once-fine farmhouse, a lone rocker sits forlorn and empty, its movement stilled, its memories lingering in happier days, while the gin machinery and silos rust in the spring showers, and the plows and water pumps sit idle, corroding in the dew. In lower Caddo Parish, we begin to bid farewell to the pervasive farm life of rural south LA 1. There are still some productive cotton fields. But here in the midst of the cotton patch, from the snowy fields white with cotton bolls sprout those unexpected metallic intrusions called "Christmas trees," series of valves controlling the flow of oil, and rhythmic pumpers going up and down, up and down, and

even a few towering derricks. The cotton field begins to give way to the oil field.

Yet, the past has not been altogether forsaken here. The historic home that traditionally graced Caspiana Plantation has been moved, incredibly all in one piece, up the road to the LSU-S campus at the southern entrance to Shreveport as the centerpiece of a little cluster of mid-1800 structures called Pioneer Heritage Village.

C.M. Hutchinson & Son

Shreveport

From the flat roadbed of LA 1, shimmering in the heat, the incredible high-rises and boomtown casinos of big, busy, bustling Shreveport suddenly rise up, like a miraculous mirage or an unexpected oasis in the desolate desert. This is one of the largest Louisiana cities and the only really urban metropolis along this highway.

It has come a long, long way since late nineteenth-century travel writer Martha Field wrote, in the New Orleans *Daily Picayune*, "Throughout all the Red River parishes the people are possessed of much general culture and refinement. Newspapers and magazines are taken in large numbers and . . . churches and schools out-balance saloons and gambling places. There are no idlers among the young men . . . Shreveport is one of the rich and prosperous cities of the South, a railroad center and a great cotton market. It has no ambition to pose as a picturesque and romantic town . . . There are no quiet,

shady and unfrequented streets lined by grand and dingy old mansions slowly feeling for their final plunge into oblivion. The town is peopled by men who came into it poor and have grown rich in legitimate mercantile pursuits." If she could see it now! There are still plenty of churches and schools, but as for gambling places—Shreveport has some of the biggest casinos in the state, and at night their brightly colored neon signs reflected in the Red River are simply spectacular.

The prospects for prosperity along the upper Red River in Louisiana would have remained unfulfilled had it not been for one man, the legendary Capt. Henry Miller Shreve. His bronze statue overlooks the Shreveport riverfront, and every museum in the area has an exhibit detailing his exploits, from the big kid-friendly wooden boat at Sci-Port to the startling exploding logs flung mid-air with a loud BOOM when a dynamite plunger drops at the Oil

The big buildings of downtown Shreveport rise up like a miraculous mirage amidst the flat cottonfields.

The neon signs of Shreveport's casinos light up the night.

and Gas Museum. And well they should, for Shreve, steamboat captain, government engineer, and superintendent of Western River improvement, was certainly the father of Shreveport.

Shreve revolutionized steamboat design by developing the shallow-draft hull that permitted big boats to navigate Louisiana's bayous and smaller rivers. In the mid-1830s, he also cleared the Great Raft, a gigantic logjam stretching more than 160 miles along the Red River, which blocked transportation and trade north of Natchitoches. With shovels and axes and dynamite as well as the famous snag boat he designed, essentially a steamboat with jaws in the bow that drew logs into a sawmill on deck, Shreve opened navigation at the same time he and a group of seven businessmen formed the Shreve Town Company and acquired the town site from Larkin Edwards, an interpreter for the native Caddo Indians. The Caddos were divested of a million acres of land by the United States government for a payment of $80,000 and a stipulation that the Native Americans would leave Louisiana; they eventually occupied reservations in Oklahoma.

Agriculture was the early economic mainstay of the Shreveport area, but with the coming of the railroads, it was soon supplanted by the lumber indus-

Webb and Webb Plantation Commissary

try. Both were eventually eclipsed by the oil boom. The Pioneer Heritage Center on the LSU-Shreveport campus presents a good picture of early life in the area. The centerpiece is the Caspiana Plantation House, built in 1856 by William Joseph Hutchinson, with historic dependencies clustered around the main house. The Thrasher Cabin is a dog-trot log structure dating from 1835, and other buildings include a log blacksmith shop, the Webb and Webb Plantation Commissary, and a doctor's office complete with old-time equipment and patent medicines. Tours are by appointment; several special-event days present living history demonstrations of such necessary skills as weaving and needlework, and there is a smithy and even an antebellum-era surgeon whose techniques either cured the patient or scared him to death.

The free Louisiana State Exhibit Museum is located at the state fairgrounds in a unique circular structure combining neoclassical and modern design, enlivened by artist Conrad Albrizio's huge colorful frescoes. Featured here are eighteen incredibly life-like dioramas created painstakingly from beeswax by one of the museum's early directors, Dr. Henry Brainerd Wright. The Poverty Point diorama recreates the most important prehistoric Native American settlement in the Mississippi Valley, built

Caspiana Plantation House

Louisiana State Exhibit Museum

from the thirties, when the Red River Valley and Mississippi Delta produced the bulk of Louisiana's cotton, which was picked by hand; not until the 1950s did modern farming methods and mechanization begin to replace manpower and mules on the small cotton farms. Today, one mechanical harvester can do the work of 150 men. In incredible detail, other dioramas replicate early agriculture and industry, and also pay tribute to the abundance of wildlife in this Sportsman's Paradise. An early doctor's buggy stands in the aisle before glassed showcases filled with Indian basketry and pottery, Civil War relics, and political displays; there is also a fourteen-foot topographical map of Louisiana. As a Smithsonian Affiliate, the museum hosts periodic traveling exhibits from the institution as well as from the office of the Louisiana Secretary of State, which also oversees Shreveport's Spring Street Historical Museum in the city's oldest building and the McNeill Street Pumping Station Water Works Museum with nineteenth-century steam equipment.

between 1,500 and 600 BC in northeast Louisiana, and this museum contains a number of significant artifacts unearthed there as well as replicas of the July 1, 1835, treaty removing the Caddo Nation from northeast Louisiana.

The diorama depicting cotton harvesting dates

The J. Bennett Johnston Waterway Regional Visitor Center, along the Red River opposite the riverwalk fountains and across the street from the convention center in Shreveport, tells the story through film and exhibits of the meandering Red River's history and the efforts of the U.S. Army Corps of Engineers to keep it navigable. Archeological artifacts from the nineteenth-century side-wheeler steamboat *Kentucky*, sunk in the river a century and a half ago, are on display, as are interesting exhibits explaining the workings of the locks and dams that keep the Red viable for travel, trade, and recreation today.

Next door, the Sci-Port Discovery Center works off the WOW factor, encouraging visiting youngsters to experience the Wonders of the World through ninety-two thousand square feet of fun interactive science exhibits, workshops, demonstrations, a planetarium, and an IMAX dome theater. "Tell me and I forget. Teach me and I may remember. Involve me and I learn," Benjamin Franklin's philosophy is quoted on the entrance panel, while the reverse side quotes Albert Einstein: "The important thing is not to stop questioning." That is the whole point here, to encourage exploration and learning, and the center's goal is to provide an educational and entertaining environment for exploring and participating actively in the world of science and technology. Static electricity demos provide a hair-raising lesson, while Mr. Bones the skeleton pedals his bicycle to show the motion of bones and muscles. The Red River Gallery lets children build a riverbank, steer a riverboat like Captain Shreve, and even observe live baby alligators. The Lucent Physical Sciences Gallery features the formation of a tornado and a pedal-powered hair drier, while nearly three hundred other hands-on interactive exhibits explore everything from fingerprints to heartbeats, from shadows to the speed of pitched baseballs. Kids can pilot a plane or land the space shuttle. The five-story IMAX theater features larger-than-life films, while the open-access interactive Sawyer Space Dome Planetarium employs the latest in projection system laser technology to make the universe come alive. There is a big Foucault Pendulum constantly swinging to illustrate the rotation of the earth; the arc of the pendulum remains on the same plane, not changing direction, and what is actually turning is the earth on its axis.

Other interesting museums in Shreveport include the Multicultural Center of the South, celebrating the area's rich cultural diversity; the R.W.

Sci-Port Discovery Center

Red River Gallery in Sci-Port Discovery Center

Norton Art Gallery with its impressive collection of western art by Frederic Remington and Charles Russell; the Southern University Museum of Art with its fine African collection; Meadows Museum of Art at Centenary College; and the Stage of Stars and Legends Music Museum in Municipal Auditorium, where Elvis made his debut at the Louisiana Hayride. The Barnwell Garden and Art Center overlooks the Red River and Riverfront Park. The Ark-La-Tex Antique and Classic Vehicle Museum features classic cars, while the Ark-La-Tex Mardi Gras Museum showcases carnival costumes. The wonderful 1920s opera house called The Strand has been restored and continues to host touring productions and extravaganzas.

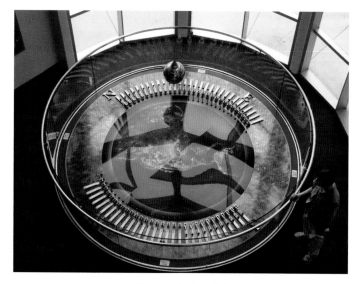

Foucault Pendulum

The Gardens of the American Rose Center, home of the American Rose Society, boast dozens of beds containing more than twenty thousand new and old-favorite specimens in every color, shape, and size. There is a lovely little chapel, fountain, carillon tower, serene Japanese tea garden, and paved walkways traversing the plantings beneath towering pines. Created in 1974, the park covers 118 acres, and it is elaborately lighted each Christmas season as part of the Holiday Trail of Lights from Natchitoches through Tyler, Texas.

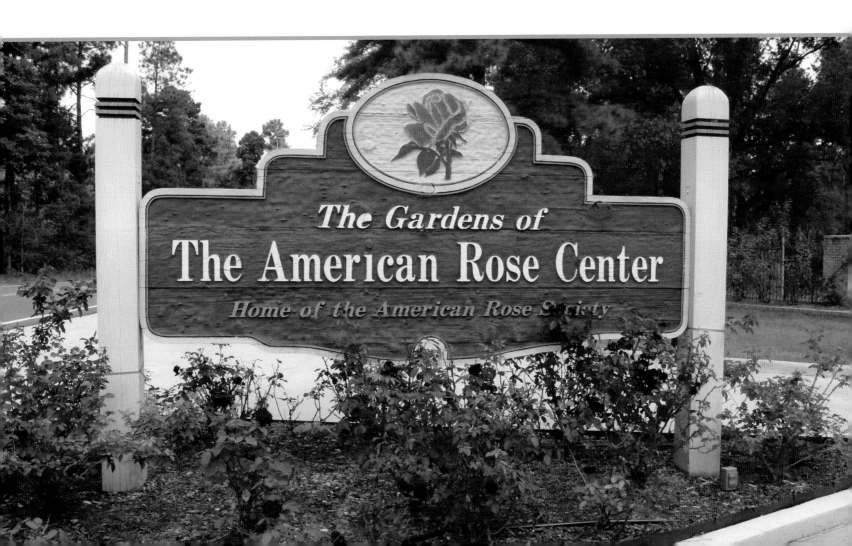

Bossier City

Shreveport was incorporated in 1839, after the clearing of the Great Raft opened exploration and trade to the area in the 1830s. Across the river, Bossier City got its start soon after as a small trading post called Cane's Landing. Incorporated and renamed in 1907, Bossier City came into its own in 1933 with the establishment of Barksdale Air Force Base, a key air combat command base and a major source of regional employment with more than ten thousand military and civilian jobs. It took 150 men and 350 mules to clear and grade the former cotton fields for the new landing fields, and the twenty-two thousand-acre base was the world's largest when it opened. It was named for World War I pilot Lt. Eugene H. Barksdale of the U.S. Army Air Corps, who perished while flight testing a new observation aircraft in 1926. (When his parachute was severed by the brace wires attached to the wings of his Douglas airplane, he fell to his death.) The "Mighty Eighth" Air Force of World War II fame is headquartered here, along with the 2nd Bomb Wing and other groups. Over the years, the base was used by pursuit and fighter crews, bomber crews, and even the combat aircraft participating in the Louisiana Military Maneuvers leading up to World War II, including the famous 17th Bomb Group led by Gen. Jimmy Doolittle during the raid on Tokyo. The base remains on the cutting edge in the twenty-first century as headquarters of the Global Strike Command to oversee the Air Force's nuclear arsenal.

Barksdale is the home base for most of the U.S. Air Force's fleet of B-52 StratoFortresses, the heavy

An immense B-52 on display at Barksdale dwarfs the tiny Russian MIG beneath its wing.

long-range bombers first flown in 1954 and still useful due to their reliability and versatility. More recently, in Vietnam, Operations Desert Shield and Desert Storm, the Persian Gulf War, and in Iraq and Afghanistan, B-52s from Barksdale have played major roles. One of these immense planes rests on display at Barksdale's Eighth Air Force Museum, dwarfing the tiny Russian MIG fighter beside it. These warplanes were front-line weaponry during the Cold War, since the B-52s were the first planes capable of carrying nuclear weapons into Russia and the MIGs would have been deployed to try to shoot them down. The museum's collection includes a number of vintage planes, including a B-17 Flying Fortress.

Today, Bossier City has its share of gaming opportunities, like Shreveport, as well as the famous Louisiana Downs racetrack.

Caddo Lake and Oil City

Seventeen miles northwest of Shreveport is beautiful Caddo Lake, nearly sixteen miles long and studded with picturesque moss-hung cypress trees like the swamplands along the southern end of LA 1. The lake was one of several natural reservoirs formed by overflow caused by the Great Raft clogging the Red River prior to the 1830s. Years of erosion along the Red washed away banks and caused large trees to fall into the water, where they drifted downriver until collected on sandbars. The legendary logjam called the Great Raft stretched for more than 160 miles and was said to be so thick in places that people could walk across it or even ride a horse-drawn carriage across. Besides blocking navigation, the raft acted as a natural dam, with river waters overflowing into low-lying spots to form Lake Bistineau, Soda Lake, Cross Lake, and Black Lake, as well as Caddo Lake. Straddling the Texas-Louisiana line, today Caddo Lake is a popular fishing spot, especially for record largemouth bass, and the lakeside park offers the perfect vantage point to watch the setting sun paint the still lake waters in brilliant hues.

Caddo Lake is also the location of the first oil well built over water. (The first well over water out of sight of land was erected some years later off the Gulf Coast near Morgan City.) After the discovery of the Evangeline Field near Jennings in 1901, wildcatters descended on the Oil City area, with the Caddo discovery, and the north Louisiana oil boom was in full swing by 1906. Early oil exploration activity strongly resembled water well drilling, and wooden oil derricks, their long support legs hoisting drilling equipment, sprouted like trees in an overgrown forest. Without the environmental or safety controls that would come later, these early wells wasted enormous amounts of natural gas daily. There were fires and explosions, and one well near Oil City burned out of control for five years, leaving a crater ninety feet deep and three hundred feet wide.

Some twenty-five thousand transient oilfield workers descended upon Oil City, living in makeshift tent cities and rustic housing. The first wildcat town in northwest Louisiana, it was a lawless boomtown filled with rowdy roughnecks, saloons, gambling dens, and a notorious ten-acre red-light district called Reno Hill. The price of land in this oil-rich

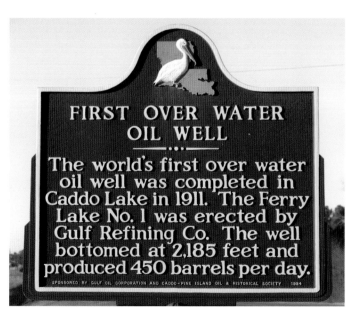

SCENIC VIEW
of
CADDO LAKE 1923

Roughnecks climb a big wooden derrick in the Oil and Gas Museum.

scenes—a big wooden derrick and the roughnecks working on it, a saloon scene with roustabouts bellied up to the bar, a typical rustic tent-house, and another early wood-frame dwelling complete with a vintage model Ford parked beside the front porch. There is also a full-scale Caddo Indian dwelling and exhibits on Native American culture and crafts in tribute to the earliest occupants of the area. Outside, there is another wood derrick surrounded by water, the old banker's house, a rustic shed with a vintage pickup, and across the railroad tracks beside the old Kansas City Southern depot, a towering metal oil derrick donated by Texaco, and lots of big early oilfield equipment. Interactive exhibits and historic photographs inside the museum make the complicated procedure of oil extraction and processing understandable, and children especially will be fascinated by the Great Raft display of real logs being dynamited at the push of a plunger to open the waterway before their very eyes.

area rose in one year from fifty cents an acre to $500 as major oil companies and private speculators vied for leases. In May 1911, Gulf Refining Company of Louisiana brought into Caddo Lake Ferry No. 1, the world's first offshore oil well, a development that would drastically alter the future of oil exploration and of the economy of the state of Louisiana as well. The well was 2,185 feet deep and produced 450 barrels a day.

One of the weathered cypress pilings from the Ferry No. 1 rig is on display at the Louisiana State Oil and Gas Museum in Oil City, a state-of-the-art 12,000-square-foot facility housing life-sized replicas of typical early

Outside the Oil and Gas Museum, a wooden derrick is surrounded by water.

❧ RODESSA ❧

This little LA 1 town was first given the rather unusual name of Frog Level because of the audible croaking coming from a nearby frog pond during a town meeting called to name the community in the 1800s. In 1898, after the railroad had come to town, the name was changed to the rather more melodic Rodessa in honor of the daughter of the Kansas City Railroad president. In the 1930s, the L.L. Young Gas Well was brought in, and Rodessa became one of the state's major oil fields.

FROG LEVEL
Later Rodessa
"History"
FROG LEVEL AND RODESSA

A TOWN MEETING WAS CALLED IN THE 1800'S BY NOAH TYSON SR., STORE OWNER, POLICE JUROR AND POST MASTER, TO NAME THEIR TOWN. THE FROGS WERE HOLLERING IN A NEARBY POND. A MAN FROM ALABAMA JUMPED UP AND SAID, "LET'S NAME IT FROG LEVEL." AND SO THEY DID. ON APRIL 11, 1879, M.C. SPEARMAN WAS APPOINTED POST MASTER. FROG LEVEL'S NAME WAS CHANGED TO RODESSA IN 1898 WHEN THE K.C.S. RAILROAD WAS BUILT IN THIS AREA. THE PRESIDENT OF THE K.C.S. NAMED THE TOWN AFTER HIS DAUGHTER, WE'RE TOLD. IN JULY OF 1935 THE I.L. YOUNG GAS WELL WAS BROUGHT IN BY UNITED GAS COMPANY, OPENING ONE OF LOUISIANA'S MAJOR OIL FIELDS. AS OF JANUARY 1, 1973, 101,773,804 BARRELS OF CRUDE OIL HAVE BEEN PRODUCED ON THE LOUISIANA SIDE.

Just up the road is the U.S. Coast & Geodetic Survey Triangulation Station marker, atop a small cement post at roadside by an abandoned gas station, where three states meet: Louisiana, Texas and Arkansas. Beyond that, LA 1 crosses the border to become a Texas highway, and our journey is done.

It would be possible to make the journey along LA 1 in a single day, from sunrise over the gentle waves of the Gulf of Mexico to sunset among the cypress trees on Caddo Lake. But this wonderful roadway, Louisiana's longest street, traverses all the diverse subregions that compose the state's geographical and cultural mosaic; hence, to rush along the route, ignoring the myriad lush landscapes, would do injustice to the richness of the journey. And after all, as they say, life's all about the journey, not simply the destination. Slow down and savor the trip.

Sunset over cypress-studded Caddo Lake

Tourist Information

Louisiana Office of Tourism
225-342-8119
www.LouisianaTravel.com

Down the Bayou

Lower Louisiana Highway One
985-448-4405
www.la1coalition.org

Grand Isle Tourist Commission
2757 LA Hwy. 1
Grand Isle, LA 70358
985-787-2997
www.grand-isle.com

Jefferson Convention & Visitors Bureau
1221 Elmwood Park Blvd., Suite 411
New Orleans, LA 70123
877-572-7474
www.experiencejefferson.com

Lafourche Parish Tourist Commission
4484 LA Hwy. 1
Raceland, LA 70394
877-537-5800
www.visitlafourche.com

Ascension Parish Tourist Commission
6967 LA Hwy. 22
Sorrento, LA 70778
888-775-7990
www.ascensiontourism.com

Madewood Plantation
4250 Highway 308
Napoleonville, LA 70390
985-369-7151
www.madewood.com

Historic Donaldsonville Museum
318 Mississippi St.
Donaldsonville, LA 70346
225-746-0004
www.historicdonaldsonville.org

River Road African American Museum
406 Charles St.
Donaldsonville, LA 70346
225-474-5553
http://www.africanamericanmuseum.org/

Attakapas Adventures Swamp Tour
1324 LA Hwy. 401
Napoleonville, LA 70390
985-369-8588
www.attakapasadventures.com

Capital

Avoyelles Commission of Tourism
8592 LA Hwy. 1
Mansura, LA 71350
800-833-4195
www.travelavoyelles.com

Iberville Parish Tourism Information Center
23405 Church St.
Plaquemine, LA 70764
225-687-2642
www.ibervilleparish.com

Plaquemine Lock State Historic Site
57730 Main St.
Plaquemine, LA 70764
877-987-7158
http://www.crt.state.la.us/Parks/iPlaqlock.aspx.

Iberville Museum
57735 Main St.
Plaquemine, LA 70764
225-687-7197

Pointe Coupée Parish Office of Tourism
500 Main St.
New Roads, LA 70760
255-638-3998
www.pctourism.org

West Baton Rouge Convention & Visitor Bureau
2750 N. Westport Dr.
Port Allen, LA 70767
800-654-9701
www.westbatonrouge.net

West Baton Rouge Museum
845 North Jefferson Ave.
Port Allen, LA 70767
225-336-2422
www.westbatonrougemuseum.com

Poplar Grove Plantation
3142 North River Rd.
Port Allen, LA 70767
225-344-3913
www.poplargroveplantation.com

Marksville State Historic Site
837 Martin Luther King Dr.
Marksville, LA 71351
318-253-8954
http://www.crt.state.la.us/parks/iMarksvle.aspx

Tunica-Biloxi Museum
150 Melancon Dr.
Marksville, LA 71355
800-488-6674
www.tunica.org/museum

Parlange Plantation
8211 False River Rd.
New Roads, LA
225-638-8410

Pointe Coupée Parish Museum
8348 False River Rd.
New Roads, LA
225-638-7788

Alexandria-Pineville Convention and Visitors
Bureau
707 Main St.
Alexandria, LA 71301
800-551-9546
www.louisianafromhere.com

City of Pineville
910 Main St.
Pineville, LA 71360
318-445-7163
www.pineville.net

Alexandria Zoological Park
3016 Masonic Dr.
Alexandria, LA 71301
318-473-1143 ext. 10
www.thealexandriazoo.com

Kent Plantation House
3601 Bayou Rapides Rd.
Alexandria, LA 71303
318-487-5998
www.kenthouse.org

Louisiana History Museum
503 Washington St.
Alexandria, LA 71301
318-487-8556
www.louisianahistorymuseum.org

Arna Bontemps African American Museum
1327 3rd St.
Alexandria, LA 71301
318-473-4692
www.arnabontempsmuseum.com

Louisiana Maneuvers and Military Museum
409 F St., Camp Beauregard
Pineville, LA 71360
318-641-8333
www.la.ngb.army.mil/dmh/immm.htm

Kisatchie National Forest
2500 Shreveport Highway
Pineville, LA 71360-2009
318-473-7160
http://www.fs.fed.us/r8/kisatchie/

Natchitoches Area Convention & Visitors Bureau
781 Front St.
Natchitoches, LA 71457
800-259-1714
www.natchitoches.net

Grand Ecore Visitor Center
106 Tauzin Island Rd.
Natchitoches, LA 71457
318-354-8770

Old Courthouse Museum
600 2nd St.
Natchitoches, LA
318-357-2270
www.lsm.crt.state.la.us/natch1.htm

Natchitoches Festival of Lights
800-259-1714
www.christmasfestival.com

Cane River National Heritage Area
452 Jefferson St.
Natchitoches, LA 71457
318-356-5555
www.caneriverheritage.org

Natchitoches National Fish Hatchery
615 South Dr.
Natchitoches, LA 71457
318-352-5324
www.fws.gov/natchitoches

Fort St. Jean Baptiste State Historic Site
155 Rue Jefferson
Natchitoches, LA 71457
318-357-3101
http://www.crt.state.la.us/Parks/iftstjean.aspx

Melrose Plantation
Association for the Preservation of Historic Natchitoches
3533 LA Hwy. 119
Natchitoches, LA 71457
318-379-0055
http://www.caneriverheritage.org/main_file.php/melrose.php/

Cane River Creole National Historical Park
400 Rapides Dr.
Natchitoches, LA 71457
318-352-0383
www.nps.gov/cari

Louisiana Pecans
208 Little Eva Plantation
Cloutierville, LA 71416
800-737-3226
www.louisianapecans.com

Natchitoches Pecans
439 Little Eva Road
Cloutierville, LA 71416
800-572+5925
www.natchitochespecans.com

Alligator Park
308 Old Bayou Pierre Rd.
Natchitoches, LA 71457
877-354-7001
www.alligatorpark.net

Shreveport

Shreveport/Bossier Convention & Tourist Bureau
629 Spring St.
Shreveport, LA 71101
888-45-VISIT
www.shreveport-bossier.org

Louisiana State Oil and Gas Museum
200 S. Land Ave.
Oil City, LA
318-995-6845
http://www.sos.louisiana.gov/tabid/242/Default.
aspx

The Gardens of the American Rose Center
8877 Jefferson Paige Rd.
Shreveport, LA
318-938-5402
www.ars.org

Sci-Port Discovery Center
820 Clyde Fant Parkway
Shreveport, LA 71101
318-424-3466
www.sciport.org

Louisiana State Exhibit Museum
3015 Greenwood Rd.
Shreveport, LA 71109
318-632-2020
http://www.sos.louisiana.gov/tabid/241/Default.
aspx

Pioneer Heritage Center
LSU-Shreveport
Shreveport, LA 71115
318-797-5339
www.ce.lsus.edu/CatalogProgramView.
aspx?ProgramID=6

Eighth Air Force Museum
99 Shreveport Rd.
Barksdale AFB, LA 71110
318-456-5553
www.8afmuseum.net

J. Bennett Johnston Waterway Regional Visitor
Center
700 Clyde Fant Parkway
Shreveport, LA 71101
318-677-2669

Anne Butler

Anne Butler is the author of a number of books—crime books, children's books, cookbooks, and humor books—and hundreds of magazine and newspaper articles, but her passion is the preservation of Louisiana's unique history and culture, as may be seen in the text for this book on Louisiana's earliest statewide roadway. She has a BA in English from Sweet Briar College in Virginia and an MA in English from Humboldt State in California. She lives on one of English Louisiana's early plantations, historic Butler Greenwood Plantation, near St. Francisville, where she writes, gives house tours, operates a Bed & Breakfast, and is involved in many preservation efforts.

Henry Cancienne

Photographer Henry Cancienne resides near the small town of Lockport in Lafourche Parish, Louisiana. Cancienne earned Bachelor's and Master's degrees from Nicholls State University in the Sciences and Education. USAF Vietnam veteran, retired educator, petroleum chemist, fireman and police officer, Cancienne has travelled extensively throughout the country, recording images of iconic locations like Niagara Falls, Yosemite National Park, Mt. Whitney and Mt. McKinley. But his passion lies much closer to home and he has photographed his native Louisiana for many decades, finding inspiration in the cypress swamps and sugar cane fields, the bald eagles of Bayou Lafourche, the butterfly shrimp trawlers, the weathered Creole and Acadian cottages and magnificent plantations, gulf beaches, and the interesting people encountered along the way. His photographic skill and superb composition enhance the natural beauty of the unique Louisiana landscape with its diverse flora and fauna. He has recently had major photo exhibits in the libraries of Houma, Lockport, Zachary, Galliano, and Baton Rouge. His exhibits were also presented at Southdown Plantation, Butler-Greenwood Plantation, Parlange Plantation, Jean Lafitte National Park, and at St. Francisville cultural centers. Henry Cancienne's photographs have been published in *Southern Breeze*, *Country Discoveries*, *Country Roads*, *Jewish Living*, various local newspapers, tourist brochures, and are featured in several forthcoming books.